"Our world is fallen and broken, but there is hope—hope in Christ for eternity beyond all pain and sorrow. Kim Meeder inspires us to believe and follow the God who transcends our limits and calls us to venture forward, with the confidence of knowing that He has our best interests in mind."

Jim Daly, president, Focus on the Family

"In *Encountering Our Wild God*, Kim Meeder has the amazing ability to use words to create a beautiful canvas that depicts God's love in its entirety. Every page glistens with the fresh dew of the Holy Spirit's presence, along with Kim's sentiment of 'Pray, Listen and Do' echoing from beginning to end. Be refreshed, comforted, then challenged to receive, recover and reclaim God's amazing promises for your life."

Lorin and Patty Carmichael, founders,
Sure Foundation Church, Puna, Hawaii

"Kim's masterful language in *Encountering Our Wild God* shows not only a life immersed in continual wild devotion to the Spirit, but a lifestyle that flows directly from that wildly wonderful place. Her book is a very not-boring devotional of sorts that colorfully illustrates the rich personality of our precious God, who rules the universe perfectly and yet is incredibly enjoyable to be with. This book will upgrade the color of your life from drab to brilliant by connecting you to the wildly adventurous Holy Spirit in a way that is reachable for all who immerse themselves in its pages."

Jennifer Eivaz, executive pastor, Harvest Christian
Center, Turlock, California; founder, Harvest Ministries
International; author, *The Intercessors Handbook*
and *Seeing the Supernatural*

"Poignantly written with a creative ease, author and horse-woman Kim Meeder becomes a life coach, a friend and a spiritual tour guide. She reveals the eternal lessons hidden within the beauty of everyday life. *Encountering Our Wild*

God will capture your attention and hold you until you begin to see the wonder of a God who pursues us relentlessly."

Dr. Wayne Cordeiro, president,
New Hope Christian College

"Kim has written this powerful book, inviting each reader to encounter God on each page. Be ready to experience God's presence as you join her insightful and fun writing! What an awesome *encounter* waits for you in this book!"

Sarah Bowling, founder, Saving Moses

"I once heard it said that God is more willing to speak to us and lead us than we are willing to listen and be led. If that is indeed accurate, then I suspect many of us are missing out on God's glorious plan for our lives. But what is that plan, and how can we discover it? *Encountering Our Wild God* is a powerful and compelling new book that speaks deeply to who God truly is, what His plan and purpose is for our lives and how we can experience and revel in His magnificence. Get ready for the ride of your life. Thank you, Kim Meeder, for showing us the way to Him!"

Frank Sontag, founder, Kingdom Men's Gathering

"The moment I read the title of Kim's new book, I was in. I *live* for life-altering encounters with the Holy Spirit. Yet I was not prepared for the deep heart journey ahead of me as I dove into *Encountering Our Wild God*. The way Kim so effortlessly pours out her wisdom, experiences and stories pulled me in for days and opened my eyes of faith to see and understand more clearly how we have this unimaginable opportunity to intimately know our untamable Creator and partner with Him in the adventure of knowing and demonstrating His heart for humanity. We will never reach the end of His nature or His love. This will be a book I revisit over and over."

Meredith Andrews Sooter, worship leader/songwriter

Encountering Our
Wild God

Encountering Our Wild God

Ways to Experience His Untamable Presence Every Day

KIM MEEDER

Chosen

a division of Baker Publishing Group
Minneapolis, Minnesota

© 2018 by Kim Meeder

Published by Chosen Books
11400 Hampshire Avenue South
Bloomington, Minnesota 55438
www.chosenbooks.com

Chosen Books is a division of
Baker Publishing Group, Grand Rapids, Michigan

Printed in the United States of America

ISBN 978-0-8007-9885-7

Library of Congress Control Number: 2017963661

Unless otherwise indicated, Scripture quotations are from the *Holy Bible*, New Living Translation, copyright © 1996, 2004, 2015 by Tyndale House Foundation. Used by permission of Tyndale House Publishers, Inc., Carol Stream, Illinois 60188. All rights reserved.

Scripture quotations identified NIV are from the Holy Bible, New International Version®. NIV®. Copyright © 1973, 1978, 1984, 2011 by Biblica, Inc.™ Used by permission of Zondervan. All rights reserved worldwide. www.zondervan.com

Scripture quotations identified NKJV are from the New King James Version®. Copyright © 1982 by Thomas Nelson, Inc. Used by permission. All rights reserved.

Scripture quotations identified KJV are from the King James Version of the Bible.

In some of the author's stories, the names and identifying details of certain individuals have been changed to protect their privacy.

Cover design by Darren Welch Design

19 20 21 22 23 24   8 7 6 5 4

As if in a dream, I walked with my hands stretched out into the unknown, still reaching for the more that is Him.

Like the apostle Philip, miraculously sent from a faraway land, you reached through the haze of unknown pursuit and firmly took my hand. You were abundantly clear that the message you bore was not your own—but from God the Father—to me.

In the brief mentoring season that followed, you led me step for loving step in the direction He was calling. Your singular purpose was to speak His encouragement over every purposeful advance in my developing faith. His words poured through you like pure light, fully illuminating the way, the way of absolute trust in following His Holy Spirit.

I watched in wonder as you removed the hallowed mantle placed upon your own shoulders . . . and draped it over mine.

And then, as quickly as you came, you were Spirited away to your next holy assignment from the Father.

Because of your obedience, this book is dedicated to God the Father, through Jesus the Son, by the power of the Holy Spirit, in honor of JLB. Thank you, dear friend, for this priceless gift.

Contents

Foreword

I love a good story. I bet you do too. Well, you are in luck, because in these pages, you are in the presence of an eloquent storyteller. We learn from stories. And in these pages, you will learn as well. Kim speaks straight to the heart as she weaves stories of her life with the intricate detail of a master craftsman. The beauty of the truth—the infinite love of God and the astoundingly magnificent offer of the Gospel—comes shining through.

I love learning from men and women who are pursuing Jesus with all their hearts, hearts that have been captured by the sacred romance of our great God with His people. Kim's heart has been captured, her life humbly surrendered, and she lives with an intimate communion with the Holy Spirit that is so alluring. It is an intimacy that we are meant to experience as well.

Kim follows the instruction of the Holy Spirit to "Pray, Listen, Do" in such a way that it ignites a fire in my heart to do the same. We get to hear from God? We get to follow

His gentle nudges? We get to live a life of extraordinary meaning? Yes, we do.

We get to live in the Presence of God every moment of our lives! How wonderful is that? Dear one, God is present in your life. He is present in this very moment, and He is present in these pages.

Read them and be invited to the wildest adventure of all—living moment by moment in partnership with the most wonderful Person you will ever know.

Stasi Eldredge, bestselling author, *Becoming Myself*;
co-author (with John Eldredge), *Captivating*
and *Love and War*

Preface

Recently, I took a dozen of my women staff to a remote waterfall in the Pacific Northwest. The rain did not stop us from enjoying the short serpentine hike that wound through a glorious temporal rainforest. Every shade of green was on display. Each bough, blade and branch was adorned with a dazzling array of droplets.

Without warning, the meandering trail led to an abrupt cliff. A very narrow bridge spanned a plunging chasm. The bridge—only 3 feet wide and 240 feet long—was hanging suspended from heavy cables. It dangled precariously in midair about a hundred feet above a second adjoining river below.

Because the bridge was suspended, every step produced movement. Lots of steps equaled lots of movement. Although the bridge was intriguing, what fascinated me most was how the beauty and power of the falls could not be seen—unless you dared to walk out onto the swaying bridge.

Each of my team encountered the bridge crossing in a unique way. Some could not wait to see how much they could rock it, while others crawled across with a white-knuckled grip on the railing. No matter what she experienced, everyone who crossed was highly aware of the vulnerability in this place and the need to *trust* the way. Each understood that she could never truly experience the waterfall until she crossed the dangling bridge and hiked down to the base, where the water thundered onto the rocks.

Once at the bottom of the chasm, we dared to walk out onto a slippery peninsula of stony basalt. This black protrusion enabled us to reach within twenty feet of where the waterfall crashed into the canyon floor. Prior heavy rains had turned the falls into a roaring wall of water that produced so much concussive force that its vibration could be felt inside your chest. Pure white authority fell with such might that it created a backwind powerful enough to carry the splash and spray straight back up into the atmosphere. In minutes, we were soaked all the way through every piece of clothing we wore. It was awe-inspiring.

Not until the return trip back over the high swaying bridge did the Lord start to give clarity.

God's plan was never for us to observe Him from a safe distance, tucked away in a dry, comfortable place. I have already done that for a season of my life. He is not looking for "spiritual tourists."

Not only does God want us to know about Him, but He desires for us to *want* to experience Him—to be soaked all the way through by His presence, to move so close to Him that we feel the vibration of His heart beating within our own.

He beckons us to pursue Him beyond our circumstances, beyond our emotions, beyond our comfort and beyond our logic. God wants us to trust Him enough to follow the leadership of His Spirit across the tenuous bridge of our human understanding and into the glorious mystery that is Him.

14

His love draws us to walk over what looks impossible—far beyond our comfort and our control—while suspended only by our trust in Him.

He is calling each of us to move through our fear and pride and to cross the swaying bridge of our unknown into the wonder of His all-known.

An African pastor by the name of Surprise declares, "The Holy Spirit is like a great and mighty river. You do not tell the river where to go. No, you do not do this. Instead, you jump into the river . . . and you go where He takes you."

The wild beauty and glory of our God is calling as He encourages us to run and jump into the awesome adventure of His ever-flowing Spirit.

Nothing within the reaches of human understanding can contain anything that He is. All He is, is unstoppable, uncontainable, unfathomable and untamable. God beckons any heart who will dare to trust Him into the extreme realm of His miraculous presence. He is not calling us to fully understand Him—He is calling us to fully *trust* Him.

This trust draws us to move beyond the seemingly safe viewpoint of observing Him from afar and to travel deeper into His presence. In this hallowed and wild place, we will see His face reflected in the miraculous—we will experience the limitless nature of our untamable God.

Acknowledgments

A special thank-you to my beloved husband, Troy; my treasured friend and traveling assistant, Judy; my cherished adventure buddy, Sue; and my incredible staff at Crystal Peaks Youth Ranch.

I love you all so very much.

What a profound joy to walk out this astounding life before Him with you at my side.

Introduction

While teaching at a women's conference in the Pacific Northwest, I did my best to connect with the participants between messages. Some wanted to share their own personal adventures of how their lives were similar to mine. Some wanted to lay their burdens down. Some wanted to pray. Many wanted their books to be signed.

I was engaged in a lively conversation with a group of women when another individual came rushing up. She reached in over the heads of those around me and exclaimed, "My friend might not be able to come today. She wanted to make sure that you signed her book." I noticed that the messenger was out of breath. She had been running; this was important. Still seated among the group, I balanced the tattered copy of *Hope Rising* on my knee.

While raising my pen over the page, I was stopped by the Holy Spirit. My prayer was little more than, *Lord, what is it? What do You want to say to this daughter?*

What flowed across the page beneath my pen was the worst gushy, greeting card–type poem ever written. It read something like:

I love you more than all the stars in the sky.
I love you more than all the sand by the sea.
All this love combined . . .
is the love we share . . . you and me.

Oh, my goodness, Lord. You can't be serious. This is terrible. The woman who owns this book is going to think I'm an idiot. I've never even seen her, and I'm writing a gag-atrocious poem about never-ending love?

I handed the book back to its courier. Once she grasped it, I held on for an instant, thinking, *I can still rip that page out. Lord, this is only making a fool out of both of us.*

As if in X-ray, I saw a flash of a Y shape. Intuitively, I knew one path led toward my pride, the other toward doing the will of my God.

I let the book go.

My thoughts ricocheted back to, *God embarrassing . . . us?* Then my own heart started to speak. *Kim, how about if you own this and call it what it is? You were hesitant to embarrass yourself. God is never embarrassed by His plan. He's God. He's never embarrassed—period.*

There, among the chatting women, I confessed my prideful heart silently before the Lord.

The conference concluded in the late afternoon. One at a time, I worked my way through the final line of those who wished for a hug, a prayer, a word of encouragement or a signature on a book. Within this beautiful procession of women, I noticed *a* woman. She was completely wrecked, crying uncontrollably while clutching a book to her chest. She stood hunched at the very end of the row.

Smiling, I caught her eye and pointed at her, communicating that I saw her and did not want her to leave. She nodded in haggard response. It took another 45 minutes to work my way to this distraught soul.

As the distressed woman stepped forward, I studied her. She was a mess. Her eyes were red and swollen; her cheeks and blouse were soaked with tears. Deep waves of emotion swept over her, causing her entire body to tremble. Whatever had rocked her was doing so at a foundational level.

Now, pressed against her chest was a copy of *Hope Rising*. She opened her mouth as if to speak, but said nothing. All that came out was an awkward attempt at stifling a sob. I watched in silence as a fresh flood of tears streamed down her face. Still gripping the small book to her chest, she opened the front cover.

Oh, my dear Lord! It's the "terrible poem" book. Before I could stop it, a reflex thought flickered across my mind. *Great, it was so bad you made her cry.*

Finally, when her words came to the surface, her voice carried those words on wings of pure astonishment. Her tear-filled eyes widened as she spoke. "How did you know? How did you know? How did you know!"

Her incredulous gaze filled the gap between us.

When she spoke again, her voice was thin and small. She sounded like a child who was waking up from a bad dream and was only now daring to emerge from beneath the covers of her trauma. Again, she asked, "How did you know?"

I shook my head in vague comprehension of her question.

Still holding the open book flat against her chest, without looking down, she pointed at the message. "This . . . *this* is what my mother used to pray over me . . . *every night* . . . when I was a child. Kim, how could you *know* this?"

She continued, "My mother just died, and I'm so lost without her. I feel so alone. I have been praying to Jesus and asking Him—if He's real—to please show me in a way that I know that He sees me, that He knows my heartache, that He loves . . . *me*." Her gaze fell to the floor.

I stooped down to catch her line of sight and looked up into her face. "And now, my friend, you *know* that He sees you. You *know* that you're not alone. You *know* that He loves . . . *you*."

The answer to the grieving woman's request of the Lord did not come from me—I could not have known it. I did not learn it through a college education, degree program or clinical certification. I was not endowed with this knowledge through any church group, small group, home group or local fellowship.

The response came through a simple individual who did a simple thing—believe in God when He calls us to trust in His Spirit, the Spirit who leads into *all* truth. The answer of faith came from the One who knows all things—God the Father. The one-and-only love that redeems was purchased by Jesus Christ the Son. And the clear message of hope was delivered through the utterance of the Holy Spirit.

> But you have received the Holy Spirit, and he lives within you, so you don't need anyone to teach you what is true. For the Spirit teaches you everything you need to know, and what he teaches is true—it is not a lie. So just as he has taught you, remain in fellowship with Christ.
>
> 1 John 2:27

Friend, God's will is not hidden from those who seek it. He has made a way for us not only to know His will but to know Him—by relying on His Spirit within us.

He wants us to trust Him enough to obey Him.

When we do this, we become the vessels through which He releases His purpose. The beauty, power and authority of His Spirit, the Holy Spirit, pours through us and into our present environment. Quite literally, when we discipline ourselves to obey His voice, we release His will on earth as it is in heaven.

This is when we will see and experience—literally live within—the loving, glorious, untamable nature of our God.

PART ONE

Encountering His Effortlessness

1

Wild Simplicity

Carefully determine what pleases the Lord.

Ephesians 5:10

Jesus, may Your love within *me—transform the world* around *me—for Your glory.*

Our purpose in this life is pretty straightforward.

Jesus said that the greatest thing we can do is love God and love each other. Yet often, as straightforward as this instruction is, our following footsteps seem to gum up in the mud of, *Am I going the right way? Am I doing the right thing? Am I in the right place?* We get caught in the "analysis to paralysis" of looking down instead of up. When our focus gets tangled in the weeds of challenge, it is easy for us to rely on ourselves instead of God. From this perspective, God is not truly God of our life—we are. While stuck in this trap, we are relying on ourselves for worth, value, love and position. From this place, nothing about us is anointed; it is appointed by our own sinful heart.

When our gaze lingers in a downward position, we get increasingly bound up in our circumstances. But when our gaze lingers in an upward position, we are led by His love and not rocked by the conditions we face.

The mission field is where we are, never where we go. The ministry of love is measured by our understanding of who we are in Him, not what we do for others. Genuine doing is the natural overflow of genuinely knowing who we are in Him, not the other way around.

Loving God and loving people—that is what He designed us to do. How that looks will be as unique as the face of everyone who calls Jesus Lord.

We will never fully understand the perfect balance of what God is doing in and through us. And I am grateful that He does not command us to understand or "see" His master plan; He asks us merely to trust Him for it—and that is not hard.

Often, my wise sister has encouraged me with this simple truth: "If you don't like the current picture of your situation, it only means that God isn't finished yet."

God isn't finished yet.

Every life is a masterpiece in process—and we can trust Him for every perfect brushstroke.

Trusting God for Every Step of His Master Plan in You

One of my all-time favorite movie moments takes place in *Indiana Jones and the Last Crusade*. The hero must save those he loves by crossing a bottomless chasm. It is too far to jump, and time is running out. So, choosing faith, he places his hand over his heart, closes his eyes and leans forward into oblivion. The audience gasps as his foot strikes a stone bridge so perfectly camouflaged that it was invisible. There was always a way, but he could not see it.

The simplicity of following our wild God is like that.

We might not always see the way, but it is always there. If we are willing to trust Him, to walk forward in faith, believing that every step is developing His design within and through us, we will see the brushstrokes of His perfect plan.

In 1995, my husband, Troy, and I founded Crystal Peaks Youth Ranch. Our ministry has a fourfold mission: Rescue the Equine, Mentor the Child, Offer Hope for the Family and Empower the Ministry. Throughout the past several decades, we have been involved in the rescue of more than three hundred horses. We serve about five thousand visitors each year, most of whom are children, completely free of charge. We help support struggling families with the hope of Jesus. And we have had the incredible joy of shouldering into existence approximately two hundred new ranch ministries throughout the United States and Canada, and over a dozen in foreign nations.

A few years ago, our ranch rescued a young golden mare with a severe wound on her left shoulder. Radiating from a central impact point were three very deep gashes, each measuring six inches in length. It appeared that at one time the injury had been closed with dozens of staples, nearly all of which had failed. The hideous result was a large chunk of exposed muscle, gaping wide for all to see.

The mare was brought to our attention when the family of her elderly owner contacted us. Through their grief, they shared how their father had not come in for dinner one night. When they went out to locate him, they discovered his lifeless body in her corral. He had passed away of natural causes in one of the places he treasured most—beside his horse. Found carefully standing over him was his beloved golden mare. She appeared also to be grieving the loss of the one who loved her most.

With no one left to manage her wounds, the distraught family asked if we could continue the mare's care and give her a new home. That day, the grieving mare came to live at Crystal Peaks.

We decided to name the mare Alulla because her resulting scar is somewhat star shaped. Over the years, Alulla has struggled with several unrelated lameness issues that have often kept her out of our riding program. Yet, in the hope that she would pull through and make a fine children's horse, we have continued to keep her at the ranch. With space at a premium for rideable horses, I often wondered if the ranch was the right home for her.

But God's portrait was not finished yet.

Releasing the Power of the Spirit through "Pray, Listen, Do"

Not long ago, I needed to pick up some picture frames for a project I had yet to finish. I'm learning—*learning*—to practice simplicity in following the Lord. Because my head works in simple ways, I like simple reminders such as, "Pray, listen, do."

With intention, I invite the Holy Spirit to lead, I listen for His answer and then I do what He says. Simple, right?

Lord, where should I go to buy frames today? I prayed as I climbed into my truck.

His answer was strangely immediate: *Goodwill.*

I was thrilled. Goodwill is like a giant yard sale all the time. I love it.

An hour later I was shopping the affordable aisles of the local Goodwill store. Then, having quickly found several frames, I made my way to the counter.

Not yet resounded in my heart.

I stopped and prayed again. With no instant answer, I took a few nondirected steps around the store. Then I realized this would be a great time to look for a few items of clothing for an upcoming speaking tour in a very warm climate. With little delay, I found a top and a pair of board shorts that would work well.

While moving back toward the checkout counter, again I heard a very clear, *Not yet.*

Okay, Lord, what else? I thought as I walked back toward the center of the store. Slowly, I had a strong sense that I needed to go look at picture frames again. Now, digging thoroughly through the stacks, I discovered a true treasure for my antique-loving heart. It was a small, very old frame with a rounded cover glass to make the picture slightly magnified and easier to see. *Thank You, Lord. This is beautiful,* I thought as I added it to my basket.

For a third time, I made my way to the checkout counter. Then I looked up at the rafters and asked, *Now?*

This time, I felt nothing but release. I realized it was time to purchase the random treasures I had found, so I moved into the next-in-line position.

Immediately, I heard the lone cashier declare to the customer in front of me, "Oh, I don't know how to do this transaction. I'll need to get the manager." With a slightly flustered cry for help, she called for another employee to come up and assist me and the rapidly growing line of customers.

From somewhere behind me appeared the relief checker. She was a small twentysomething woman with bright-red hair and striking blue eyes. In her hasty fluster to get to the checkout counter, she cut in front of me forcefully, nearly knocking my basket out of my hands. It did not take a genius to recognize that she was mad.

In a terse, monotone voice, she asked, "Did you find everything you needed?" It was not really a question; it sounded more like, *Back off, lady! I'm not in the mood to deal with you!*

A ringing phone stole her attention away before I could answer. While she spoke on the phone, I had a moment to study her. Even though her voice and demeanor belied that she was tired and frustrated, she was still a stunning beauty. The name tag on her blue work smock read, "Angel."

She slammed the phone down with so much force that it sounded like a shotgun. Again, she turned to me and asked in the same emotionless tone, "Did you find everything you needed?"

Hoping she would not beat me with the phone, I ventured an explanation. "Actually, I found more than what I came for. I found some clothing that I'll need for an upcoming speaking event."

Without glancing up she continued, "Great! So . . . what d'ya speak on?"

"Well," I began, "I get to speak about hope." And then I shared a brief explanation of how Crystal Peaks Youth Ranch rescues and rehabilitates horses. We then pair them with hurting kids for free. We also provide support for families and have assisted more than two hundred other ranches like ours into existence around the world.

Still with no eye contact, her dutiful response was little more than a short, exhaled, "Huh."

Feeling lost in a superficial exchange about hope, I asked the Holy Spirit, *What do You want me to say to her?*

Before the answer came, her rising frustration breached what was left of her fragile restraint. She stood up straight, rocked back on her heels and all but shouted, "I'm so glad you talk to people about hope 'cause I'm sick and tired of the fact that nobody takes responsibility for anything they do anymore. Nobody! And I'm just sick of it! I'm sick of it!"

With my hair blown back and my eyebrows closer to the ceiling, the question I had asked the Lord still hung between us. Then came His reply: *Beloved, I want you to point-blank her with what I've done for you.*

Jesus, what? Are You kidding me? This girl just yelled in my face! Lord, she's mad. She's not going to receive it. Trust me. Even the guy waiting behind me is mad. Seriously, Lord, this isn't the right time!

My scrambling resistance about timing was met with an internal silence—His smiling exclamation point on His original request.

In seconds, trust broke through resistance. A decision was made to jump into the river of the Holy Spirit and go where He wanted to flow.

Okay . . . I'm goin' in!

Leaning into the plow of "pray, listen, do," I looked directly at her fuming blue eyes. Before I spoke, my silent prayer was, *Holy Spirit, lead me.*

"Angel, I agree with you that everyone needs hope in their lives. I'll never forget the day I found genuine hope. I was nine years old. It was the same day that my dad murdered my mother and then killed himself. In my grief, I cried out to Jesus—the Author of hope—and He's been in my heart ever since."

Angel reacted as if she had suddenly been struck by an unseen arrow.

She stiffened instantly while drawing in a quick breath. Her previous passive glance in my direction crashed to the floor. With her shoulders drawn up toward her ears, she did not move; she did not breathe. She stood frozen in place, seemingly locked in time.

It felt as if minutes had gone by. Gradually, she began to exhale. Her small shoulders returned to a normal level. In what looked like slow motion, her eyes rose to meet mine.

When our gazes locked, her eyes were flooding with liquid sorrow. Before a word was spoken, two huge tears streaked down her cheeks. She began to speak. Her voice was scarcely audible. It was no longer the monotone drone of a frustrated woman. It was the high, broken plea of a little girl.

"When I was twelve," she began, barely audible, "I saw my mom kill herself right in front of me." Her nostrils flared hard. She fought to stifle a sob. Then she continued with no voice at all, "*I've never told that to anybody.*"

Without a word, I opened my arms in the universal gesture of, *This hug's for you.* Not waiting to go around the counter, she launched straight over it—right into my arms. Collapsing into the embrace of a complete stranger in the checkout line of a Goodwill store, a little brokenhearted girl was introduced to Jesus' love.

The Holy Spirit will always lead toward truth. And when truth is revealed, there is freedom.

I held her for a long time, whispering encouragements from one former orphan to another.

It was within that moment that a beautiful piece of God's profound picture dropped into my view. I leaned back from my new friend so I could look into her face.

34

"Angel, I would love to have you come to my ranch. I have a very special horse that I'd like you to meet. I think that the two of you might understand each other perhaps better than anyone could understand either one of you."

Her eyes were leveled on mine. Although still wet with tears, her eyes looked profoundly different. They looked . . . hopeful.

I continued, "Not long ago our ranch rescued a horse that watched the one person on this earth that she loved the most die right in front of her. When her master's body was discovered in her corral, she was standing over him. Even though she could not stop what happened, she still loved him very much."

The young woman before me nodded wordlessly in subconscious understanding.

Continuing to tell Angel about herself through Alulla, I proceeded, "She's a precious horse that just needs someone to help her know that she's going to be okay. Do you think you can help me with that?"

Still trying to process all that had happened, Angel blinked her beautiful eyes a few times before she responded quietly, "Yes . . . I would love that."

After a quick exchange of contact information, I walked out of the Goodwill store with my bag full of treasures. I glanced back at the real treasure standing behind the counter. She was demure, yet beaming with an unmistakable radiance.

"I'll see you soon," I called to her.

"Yes, you will," she called back.

Climbing into my truck, I realized how our all-knowing God had woven horrific threads from my life into something beautiful, something redeeming. It was His plan all along to seam together the loss of my parents, reaching out to Jesus and the rescue of a wounded, brokenhearted horse into fabric that would enfold around and bring comfort to a wounded, brokenhearted girl.

My sister was right. If we do not like the current picture of our situation—the painful parts of our life—it only means that God is not finished yet. As the Master Artist, He does not waste a single brushstroke . . . ever.

"For we are God's masterpiece. He has created us anew in Christ Jesus, so we can do the good things he planned for us long ago" (Ephesians 2:10).

So we can *do* those good things He planned for us long ago.

Our pain always has a purpose, but only when we give it to Him—all of it. When we keep our pain, it hurts. When we give our pain to Jesus, He is the One who makes it into something beautiful, something that can become the healing bridge from the brokenhearted to His heart. Only Jesus can do that.

There are no coincidences. His plans for you were forged long ago. In God's hands, not a day of your pain is ever wasted. In His timing, He will use every single one—if you're willing to trust Him while you walk *with* Him toward the completion of the masterpiece He is painting within you.

It is so easy to get entangled in all the "purpose" questions about life. But the Spirit of the living God leads each of us into "all truth" (John 16:13).

You want to know God's will for your life? Easy. You pray, you listen, you do (see Colossians 4:2; John 8:47; Ephesians 2:10).

This is the wild simplicity of our God.

ENCOUNTER HIM THROUGH *Prayer*

Lord Jesus,

I acknowledge that I wasn't created to live in my pain—I was created to live in Your presence.

I understand that my pain, when given completely to You, has a powerful purpose that gives You glory. I also understand that my pain, when kept in the dungeon of my soul, has an equally powerful purpose that steals Your glory.

In this moment, Holy Spirit, show me every painful thing that still resides within my heart. Reveal all that I haven't fully surrendered to You. Now, before You, I name them all.

In this moment, remove my pain, precious Lord, and fill the void with Your presence. Take what the enemy meant to destroy me with, and transform it into the very thing that will give the suffering souls around me life—Your life!

Jesus, heal my eyes. Help me to see my past as You see it—a strategic, beautiful, fiery forge that created within me Your loving and powerful weapons of war. Help me know that as hard as my past has been, it's what You've used to develop within me Your power to reach the lost with Your saving grace . . . and that's pain worth enduring.

Fully armed with a heart overflowing with Your healing love, lead me out into the world. Right now, I raise the banner of "pray, listen, do" over every minute of my life. On this day, I choose to forever embrace the wild simplicity that is You. Amen.

2

Wild Compassion

Devote yourselves to prayer with an alert mind
and a thankful heart.

Colossians 4:2

To experience the wild compassion of our God, we need to do only one thing—follow His lead.

"God is love" (1 John 4:16). His love surrounds us every minute of every day. We each have an inexhaustible river of love to draw from whenever we choose. Most of us will choose to flow in His love from time to time throughout our day. But here is the rub: Since His love is limitless, why do we not choose to live in it *all* the time?

I have navigated so much of my life on autopilot, moving mechanically through the more routine parts of my day. Then, when the spiritual parts arrive—meetings, speaking, praying, writing, engagements—I ask that His Spirit fill, inhabit and lead me. That is certainly a good thing, but not His best thing.

It was never God's intention for any of us to live our lives in the land of perpetually playing spiritual hokey-pokey: "I put my whole heart in. I pull my whole heart out. I put my whole heart in and shake it all about. I do the hokey-pokey, and I turn myself around. That's what it's all about!"

Trust me, that is *not* what it is all about.

Jesus did not die on the cross so we could live part-time in His river of love. He wants us to be made complete in His love.

> I pray that from his glorious, unlimited resources he will empower you with inner strength through his Spirit. Then Christ will make his home in your hearts as you trust in him. Your roots will grow down into God's love and keep you strong. And may you have the power to understand, as all God's people should, how wide, how long, how high, and how deep his love is. *May you experience the love of Christ*, though it is too great to understand fully. Then you will be made *complete* with all the fullness of life and power that comes from God.
>
> Ephesians 3:16–19, emphasis added

It is God's desire that we are so filled with His love that it sloshes out of us wherever we go (see 1 Thessalonians 3:12).

Jesus exemplified this phenomenon wherever He went. He walked in compassion every minute of every day. He traveled into the back streets, the lonely country roads and the seashores. He went to where the hurting people were. He called little children to come dive into His arms. He welcomed the throngs to crush in around Him and feel His presence. He encouraged the spiritually destitute to anoint His head and feet. He loved them all right where they were. His ministry of compassion was not where He went—it was always where He was.

How did He do it? Simple—He followed the leadership of the Holy Spirit.

What does that look like for you and me? Exactly the same.

It looks like being present in the only moment we have— the one we are living in right now.

His love is available to flow through us all the time, but are we choosing all the time to be available for His love to flow through us?

We can.

I'm 55 years old, and I'm still learning this basic principle.

Kim, just be present in His presence. Be intentional to follow the Spirit's lead in this moment. Right now, look for individuals to release His limitless compassion over.

Walking in the Awareness of His Wild Compassion

Recently, I was dashing through a very busy day when a brief opening of time allowed me to fly into the grocery store to pick up some items for dinner. I jumped out of my truck, slung my wallet on a string over my shoulder and hooked my keys on the string. Then I locked my truck, pulled my cap down tight and sprinted into the store. Total routine.

On my way through the automatic doors, the Holy Spirit spoke, *Pray for them . . . all of them.*

Hmm, okay, was my unadorned response. The only way I felt I could do a good job was to walk the entire store around the outside aisles and pray over every individual inside the building. Once I had done this, I got down to the business of shopping. I did not have a list, so I thought if I zigzagged down every aisle, my memory would be jogged when I saw what I needed. Rarely do I have enough time to shop in such a haphazard way, but this was the best I could do for this moment.

I breezed through my favorite part of the store first— produce. Yum! Then, I started to rush down each aisle. I passed a dark-haired woman who appeared to be doing the same thing, only in the opposite direction. Aisle after aisle, we kept meeting in the middle. What started out as a smile soon grew into superficial jokes.

"Hey, fancy meeting you here! Toilet paper's on sale over on aisle five! The mangoes are really good today. I saved a few for you!"

In no time, I had completed my shopping and found the shortest checkout line in the front of the store. While waiting, I was aware that the dark-haired woman was about to pass directly behind me. Suddenly, she stopped and backed up. Then she pushed her cart up next to mine and looked at me. I expected her to speak, but she stood there speechless.

I studied her. Did I know her from somewhere? Nope. She was a total stranger. Perhaps I reminded her of someone she knew?

The look in her eyes made her appear conflicted, as if she were grappling with something. Slowly, she moved forward until she was close enough to reach out and place her hand on my arm.

She started to speak twice and stopped herself both times. I could see she was struggling with what she wanted to say. Finally, she stammered, "I . . . I do not know what it is about you, but every time I was close to you . . . I felt safe . . . and I felt loved."

There in the checkout line of a local grocery store, two complete strangers embraced. They hugged for no other reason than that one felt from the other the release of our God's wild compassion.

Thanking me was all that made sense to her in that moment. She did not yet understand that she had encountered the Person of the Holy Spirit and His love for her. I was merely the vessel that bore His compassionate presence.

Looking for the "More" in Sharing His Wild Compassion

A few weeks later, my husband and I were summoned to the beautiful town of Sisters for a lunch meeting. During our drive, we had a casual discussion about what it means to be present before the Lord. Once we arrived at the little restaurant, it was easy to see that it was completely full and abuzz with happy chatter. Troy and I were seated at the last available table. Once settled in, we waited for our friends to join us.

During our wait, a very thin waitress zoomed by us several times. She looked frazzled. Soon, she dashed to our table and brought glasses of water. With a flat tone, she asked, "How's your day going?"

"Great," I responded. "How's *your* day going?"

"Okay." A look of surprise crossed her face.

"Now, there's an honest answer! *Are* you okay?"

Her gaze darted across the room in a visual check to see if she had time to answer my question. Finally, she mumbled, "I've been better." With that, she dashed away.

She was hurting.

In the chaos of the moment, I offered up a silent prayer for her.

Our friends were delayed and not able to meet us within the time frame we had scheduled, so Troy and I had an unexpected lunch date together. Throughout our meal, as often as I could, I caught eyes with the stressed waitress and spoke words of encouragement to her as she rushed by.

Then, the Holy Spirit highlighted something interesting, something He wanted me to see. As if subconsciously playing a child's game of my youth, Hot and Cold, I started to notice the weary waitress slow down as she passed our table. Inexplicably, as if walking through an unseen bog of His love, she relaxed her pace a bit more each time she walked through our presence. Fascinating! And then she passed our table, banked a hard 180-degree turn, and slid right into the booth where I was sitting. Before I could even tell my body what to do, my left hand landed in the middle of her back and started making the slow "Mama circles" of comfort.

I did not even have time to process what had happened before she started to pour out her personal heartache. Her son had died. Now she and her husband were lost in a dark cavern of grief. I told her that I knew that place. I, too, was there after the murder-suicide of my parents. But I was not there any longer because of the love of Jesus. Following the Spirit of compassion, I asked her, "Are you a praying woman?"

She looked down and spoke softly. "Sometimes."

I proceeded gently. "May I pray for you?"

Without looking up, she nodded silently.

Right there, in the middle of the lunch rush, a broken waitress leaned against the shoulder of a complete stranger as she prayed and cried.

Once our prayer was over, she dried her face with the back of her hands. While hugging me, she whispered in my ear, "Thank you, friend. You have no idea how badly I needed that." Then, she disappeared as quickly as she arrived, racing back into the fray of attending to her hungry patrons.

And just like that, the wild compassion of our God was released.

The administration of His love is not really a "where" but a "who."

Who will choose to live in the river of His mighty compassion? Who will choose to go where His love wants to flow? Who will choose to remain in Him, so much so that His limitless love is merely the overflow through them—wherever they are?

This is His desire for all who belong to Him.

When it comes to His compassion, will we choose to be present in the moment we have? His love is so mighty, so powerful, so gentle. It transforms every heart it contacts. His love is like light in the darkness. What seems small and insignificant to some can be enough—for those who are in a very dark place—to light the way toward release and freedom.

> All praise to God, the Father of our Lord Jesus Christ. God is our merciful Father and the source of all comfort. He comforts us in all our troubles so that we can comfort others. When they are troubled, we will be able to give them the same comfort God has given us.
>
> 2 Corinthians 1:3–4

The wild compassion of our God can be administered in as many ways as there are individuals who cross our daily paths. When we walk in the awareness of the overflow of His love, we will see it transform the human environment around us.

Jesus Himself said that loving God and each other is the greatest commandment (see Matthew 22:34–39). When we choose to intentionally walk in the ways of His compassion, we are set apart by the same. Because His love beams through us into the darkness, it shines in high contrast to the bitterness of this world. He desires for us to be known by His love in us (see John 13:35).

Paul wrote, "Clothe yourself with the presence of the Lord Jesus Christ" (Romans 13:14). And he also wrote this:

> Since God chose you to be the holy people he loves, you must clothe yourselves with tenderhearted mercy, kindness, humility, gentleness, and patience. Make allowance for each other's faults, and forgive anyone who offends you. Remember, the Lord forgave you, so you must forgive others. *Above all, clothe yourselves with love, which binds us all together in perfect harmony.*
>
> Colossians 3:12–14, emphasis added

What a beautiful image to aspire toward—to be "clothed," covered, literally dressed in the love of God. It is not hard. It is a choice, as simple as choosing to be present in His loving presence in every moment.

"Love never gives up, never loses faith, is always hopeful, and endures through every circumstance. . . . Three things will last forever—faith, hope, and love—and the greatest of these is love" (1 Corinthians 13:7, 13).

We need to be present to look for the "more." How can I pour more of Christ's love into those around me?

While we still have breath, you and I have a profound opportunity, a mission of epic proportion—we carry within us the limitless river of Jesus' love. Because of this sacred endowment, we can give the greatest, most life-changing and powerful gift known to humankind to every heart in our midst. And when His pure love impacts genuine brokenness, nothing in that hurting heart will ever be the same.

Friend, this is the wild compassion of our God.

ENCOUNTER HIM THROUGH *Prayer*

King Jesus,

In this moment, I'm aware of how distracted I've become. I see how I've allowed "me" and my harried schedule to move in front of Your compassion for the suffering souls around me. The enemy loves my busyness because he knows what "busy" really means: "Being Under Satan's Yoke." It's not a glamorous distraction, but it's highly effective in removing me from the front lines of spiritual warfare—the cutting edge where Your glorious sword of compassion is wielded to free the lost.

Lord, between my busyness and complacency, I recognize that I just give up way too easily on the hurting in my midst.

No more! I want my sword back. I want to return to the front lines. I want to return to the position of loving battle You created for me before the world began.

Holy Spirit, show me my "busy." Show me where You aren't first. Show me the enemy's lies within my day—I choose to submit every minute to You alone. Precious Lord, Your wild compassion is easy. When my eyes are fixed on Your face, Your love covers me like clothing.

Jesus, today I choose to grip Your sword of compassion with both hands because I know Your love never gives up. It's so powerfully pure that it cannot be confined by my loss of faith, my loss of hope or my lack of endurance. When I choose to yield all my heart to be filled and clothed with all Your compassion, that's when the world around me will be transformed by the overflow of You through me.

From this day forward, I commit my feet to You. May they run to carry Your rescuing compassion into the world to those who've collapsed in hopeless despair around me. Holy Spirit, armed with Your wild compassion, show me the "more"!

3

Wild Presence

"I know my own sheep, and they know me, just
as my Father knows me and I know the Father.
. . . They will listen to my voice."

John 10:14–16

The wild presence of our God is simply that—a presence
too extreme to describe. He is not a thing or an "it." He is
a "who," a living presence occupying space and time—but
in a vastly different way than you and I do.

This "who" lives within the heart of every soul who calls
Jesus Lord of his or her life. Often, His presence inside us
responds like fire—when we feed a flame, it grows; when we
starve a flame, it shrinks. The more we heed His voice, the
more we hear His voice. The more we rationalize His voice

as anything other than what it is, the more we reduce our ability to hear it (see John 10:1–16).

We know God inhabits the praises of His people (see Psalm 22:3). We also know that the more we praise Him and acknowledge His presence, the greater we feel the release of His presence through us. Truly, this is the point, the whole reason we live: to praise and worship Him and subsequently be filled with His presence—and then release that same beautiful presence into the world around us.

Learning to be intentional in this manner is changing my life in such a crazy, wild, powerful way. I am a 55-year-old girl who carries the presence of the living God within her. When I am fully present and intentional in each moment, His presence is released—through me—into the environments I occupy. What awe-inspiring, crazy, amazing fun this has been!

Everyone who knows me well understands that I am a woman of the wilderness. Even from early childhood, I was the last kid to the dinner table. Without fail, I would slide in from parts unknown, filthy, sweaty, with wild treasures in my pockets and a few stuck in my hair. Inspired from this season of my life, my all-time favorite quote from my beloved grandpa was, "Good Lord, kiddo! You look like you've been runnin' through the bushes to comb your hair."

He was right.

Indeed, the wilderness is where I experience God. It is my truest church, where I am most free before Him. In this hallowed place, some of His greatest gifts to my wild heart have been as unassuming as an appointed breeze, a narrow shaft of light, a heart-shaped stone, an icy dip, perfect snowflakes on my eyelashes, a deep night sky or a rare antler that reminds me of His covenant.

Purposing to Carry His Wild Presence Where He Wants to Go

Given my penchant for life in the wilderness, the opposite swing of the pendulum rings equally true. While earthly achievements and accolades are not a bad thing, they are not my thing. Troy, my blessed husband, can attest to the truth that I would rather beat down the door of my dentist's office and demand a quadruple root canal than accept a nomination to be presented at a black-tie award ceremony.

So when the call came announcing my nomination for a high-profile award, to say I was "reluctant" would be a significant understatement. Any observer would have said my reaction looked exactly the same as dragging a 165-pound dog toward the veterinarian's office.

My rant began with some *waah-waah*s that would have put any colicky baby to shame. Next, I listed every reason why this was a bad idea, including the fact that I do not even own a dress. Then, I wrangled verbally with God with all the grace of a steer wrestler. What a muddy, selfish mess I had created! Lastly, once I had made my case, I finally closed my mouth, waiting for God to agree with me.

My thoughts trailed off, and I prayed, *Okay, God, this is uncomfortable. How can it be Your will for me to be uncomfortable?*

What I felt next might best be described as Him rolling His eyeballs until they hurt. (Yes, I am pretty sure He can do that.) Then, in the sweetest and most humorous way, He reminded me, *Beloved, this award isn't about you. It's about Me. I'm choosing to position you to win this award. Then, you will have a platform to give Me glory.*

Oh. I paused. *So . . . all my selfish flailing was for nothing?*

I sensed His deepening smile. *Yup! Just sending you out in a unique way to a unique crowd. All good!*

With the selfish bluster drawn out of my sails, I moved back to the process of learning to walk in His presence—daily, continually, persistently.

Well, I responded, *all righty then.*

The next step of walking through the awards process was to sit before a distinguished panel of judges, twelve women, and answer a comprehensive battery of questions. It was my understanding that the nature of the questions would be concealed until the moment they were asked, so the response would be honest and natural.

Having little idea of what would be asked within this interview, my ultimate preparation strategy was simple: fast and pray.

Lord, it's You who's calling me to walk into this interview. I trust You to give me the words needed to bring glory to Your name.

The big day arrived with the speed and subtlety of a whip-lash. My interview was squashed within a day of meetings that were scheduled so tightly together that the person I was meeting with before the interview agreed to ride along in my truck and wait for me to finish so we could pick up where we had left off. I walked into the posh business building, ducked into the restroom and did a quick foreign object sweep, made my way to a waiting area and found a chair and sat down to await my turn.

Instinctively, I fixed my eyes on the closest window, and my view launched out and up, soaring into the brilliant blue sky. Large white clouds drifted along, free of the entrapments and expectations of men. They went with the flow—His flow. Right there in the reception area, I purposed to do the

51

exact same thing—ride the current of His presence and go wherever He wanted to go.

While I gazed intently out the window, the Holy Spirit reminded me of the gospels when Jesus was praying in the Garden. He knew what awaited Him: taking on the sin of all mankind, being separated from His Father and then dying on the cross. To say that He dreaded it would be the greatest understatement in human history. He prayed, "Father, if you are willing, please take this cup of suffering away from me. Yet I want *your* will to be done, not mine" (Luke 22:42, emphasis added). Then when the rabble came to arrest Him, He stepped *forward* to meet them (see John 18:4). The Holy Spirit reminded me that in this minor act of obedience, I could do exactly the same thing—step forward into this opportunity and speak the truth.

My appointment was scheduled for 2:00 p.m. After about twenty minutes, the door of the interviewing room opened, and a very haggard woman stepped out. Presumably, she was another nominee who had been questioned. She brushed past me, eyes down, and headed straight for the exit door.

I was next.

Once invited, I entered the room. It smelled like strong salad dressing and women who needed some fresh air. The emotional climate was clearly one of fatigue and frustration. I sensed they had been doing this for days. I was either last or near the end of their process, and they were already emotionally done. Most of the women had pushed back from a long conference table, appearing to try to find a more comfortable sitting position.

I noticed that the ladies were aligned directly across from each other in near-mirrored pairs. At the far end of the table sat a woman I have known for decades and had not seen in nearly as long. She is a community pillar and a woman I respect greatly and love even more.

I greeted her warmly, calling out her name over the shuffling as each judge gathered herself for one more interview.

Instantly, my old friend shut down the greeting in a fashion that let me know, *This is serious business, and I cannot show any emotion other than professionalism as the leader of this panel.* I smiled at her directly, silently communicating that I understood and would comply.

As if by rote, introductions were made by each judge. Most of them slumped in their chairs in the posture of someone whose tail hurt and who no longer wanted to be sitting. Some sat with their arms across their chest in a "prove why I should like you" position. One leaned forward with her elbow on the table and her chin in her hand in a universal slouch of, *Please make this meeting be over.*

They were tired. Their bodies were present, but their minds struggled to stay in the game. From any human perspective, this looked to be a lost pursuit, completely over before it started.

That is when the Holy Spirit nudged me. I could hear Him laughing in my heart. *It's a good thing that I'm not confined to any human perspective. Follow Me.*

The meeting was called to order, and the first question was lobbed. They wanted me to talk about my qualifications and what makes me such a good leader to my staff. I had to quench my urge to laugh out loud and opted instead to speak the truth. I flipped the question and told them that my staff are spectacular because they follow Jesus and walk in His love. I shared how I wanted to be more like *them* and how every day they encourage, support and inspire me. I pressed into the truth of how I am so grateful to be surrounded by a family that knows His love is the greatest gift.

The panel looked perplexed. This was clearly not what they were expecting. They asked a few clarifying questions to define the work of the ranch and the heart of what it does.

Drilling down deeper, they returned to the list and asked, "So what qualifies you to lead your organization and counsel broken children?" Although the context of this question was rooted in educational degrees and certifications, I could feel the Holy Spirit welling up. This was not a question to glorify men . . . but God.

What happened next sounded like a masterful symphony of words streaming from lips that happened to be mine. I recognized the sound of my voice, but the words were not coming from my brain. I heard a welcome embrace for such a thoughtful question. I listened, as the stage was set within my own life of the powerful bond of love between my parents and my child's heart. Then I heard myself say, "What qualifies me to work with broken children is not measured by degrees or certifications. What qualifies me to work with any broken child is simply this: I *was* that broken child. I *was* every destroyed kid that walks up our hill. This child's life was destroyed—broken into oblivion—the day her father murdered her mother and then took his own life.

"What makes this life qualified is that I did not stay in that shattered place. In that moment of utter devastation, I cried out to Jesus. I asked Him to help me. In that very instant, the Lord of love took the little hand that was reaching out to Him . . . and He has never let go. It was His unbreakable grip of love on my heart that pulled me through the flames of grief and despair. There's nothing more powerful to a soul in crisis than to hear someone say, 'You're going to be all right and here's how I know. I once was where you are—and I'm not there anymore. Come with me, let me show you the way.' Because of Him, I am alive. Because of Him, I made it through. Because of Him, I sit before you today. And that . . . is what qualifies this life."

I sensed their emotional cogs lock into place with personal gears of understanding. The atmosphere in the room was being transformed.

I could feel the Spirit being released. As the questions kept coming, the Spirit kept speaking. He spoke of what it means to be seen and heard, to belong to a family, to be counted as a beloved son or daughter. He spoke of how Jesus sees every hurt. He knows, He was present when it happened and He cares. He spoke of how every wounding can be healed and redeemed by the vast expanse of Jesus' love.

I was aware of a subtle shift. Seamlessly, we crossed over from speaking about the children at the ranch to speaking about the children inside the women in the room.

Now, I could not only feel His presence moving through our midst, but I could also see it. Beginning with the pair of women closest to me, I noticed a profound transformation.

Subconsciously, each started to lean forward, toward me. The woman on my left, whom I had never met before this day, reached out and put her hand on my arm. While I was speaking to this distinguished panel of judges, this judge started to make small circles on my arm with her thumb. Her head dipped slightly lower than mine, in a submissive posture, like a child. In that moment, my sense was that she was becoming a child and reaching out for the love that was pouring from the Spirit.

As the Holy Spirit impacted both women who were closest to me, they each started to silently cry. Clearly, He was moving forward through the room, because then the second pair of women also started to cry. Nearly on cue, the third pair of women beyond them started to cry. Then the fourth pair and the fifth pair until everyone in the room was crying—not because of the words that streamed from my mouth, but because the Spirit of love had impacted them. They were each having an encounter with Him. This interview process had nothing to do with an award; it had everything to do with the Kingdom of heaven being delivered into their presence and pouring into the hurting hearts of these adult children. It was fascinating, powerful and beautiful to watch.

By now, the list of questions had been tossed over the leader's shoulder, and they were asking thinly veiled personal questions. It was such a sweet and nurturing time.

Finally, my friend at the end of the table raised both of her hands in a palms-up position and said, "Wow, wow, wow! I don't know what else to say. That was simply amazing!" And with that, our meeting was over, and I was shown to the door.

I pushed the heavy glass exit doors outward and took a deep breath of the crisp air that rushed in around me. I had a picture of the 165-pound dog being dragged to the vet's office. Wow, this dog would have missed so much had she clung to that posture. I smiled with realization. This dog needs to not make selfish assumptions and learn to run and jump into her Master's presence and follow Him no matter where He might lead.

Pursuing His Wild Presence—So We Can Release the Same

A week after the interviews, the grand gala event was held. My dear friend Ann had gone online and ordered—for me—a beautiful black wraparound dress. As only the Lord could arrange, it fit perfectly. Troy and I fasted and prayed. Side by side, we went to the black-tie event. With our hearts open, we prayed over everyone in the building. As previously assured by the Holy Spirit, when the twentysomething names were read for the award I had been nominated for, my name was spoken as the winner. As promised by this daughter's heart, I shared the hope of the Gospel, the message of Jesus Christ, for all in attendance.

One would think this would be the end of the story. But I am learning something profound. Often, we think the Lord is doing one thing when the truth is, He is doing a thousand. Days after the award ceremony, my longtime friend who was the head judge called me out of the blue. We had not spoken face-to-face in years. How she even had my personal cell number is still a mystery. Once we walked through the brief surprise and joy of being connected, that is when the greater truth began to pour out.

She set the conversational stage by clarifying that she had been heading out of town. But she was so impressed by the weight of importance of what she wanted to share that she had pulled her car over on a mountain pass so she could deliver her message before losing cell phone reception.

Searching for the right words, she stammered, "Kim, I probably should not be telling you this . . . but . . . but . . . I have just never experienced anything like what happened during your interview. You need to know that what you said had such an impact, on all of us, that after you left, we cried for twenty minutes!"

Even in the retelling of that moment, she was laughing and crying at the same time. "We still had one more in- terview, and we used every napkin in the room to mop up and merely try to pull ourselves together after what you shared."

She continued, "I'm not really sure what happened during that time, but we were so completely shaken. We were completely *undone* when you left."

That revelation of clarity, in turn, made me laugh and cry at the same time. After we spoke of several other topics in our brief conversation, she said, "Thank you for sharing your heart. Thank you for speaking the truth. Thank you for speaking in such a way that we *all* felt the love of God."

There it was. The bigger picture was revealed.

All the hoopla surrounding this black-tie ceremony was never about an award or an interview; it was always about positioning a heart that was following the leadership of the Holy Spirit so that He would be released into a specific atmosphere. It was always about Him. I had left the room. I was no longer present. I was gone. But He remained. And once delivered, He lingered over the raw hearts of His little girls and loved them really well.

Looking back, I can see how this whole experience was actually a straightforward exercise of obedience.

Kim, when you choose to get over yourself and out of your comfort zones, that's when you'll truly see His wild presence pouring forth in beautifully unexpected ways.

As stated earlier in this chapter, the more we heed His voice, the more we hear His voice. The more we rationalize His voice as anything other than what it is, the more we reduce our ability to hear it (see John 10). We know God inhabits the praises of His people (see Psalm 22:3). We also know that the more we praise and acknowledge His presence, the greater the release of His presence through us. This is the main point, the whole reason we live: to praise and worship

Him and subsequently be filled with His presence—and then release that same beautiful presence into the world around us.

Friend, we each carry His Spirit within us. We are each accountable and responsible to deliver Him where He wants to go. We are the living vessels that carry the presence of the living God. May we purpose before Him to never quench His flow or stop His move by locking down in our own fears or pride. May we look intently, may we listen actively, may we do what He calls us to do. Thereby, our life transforms into a living testimony that proclaims He is really our God.

It is not up to us to understand every twist and turn of our journey before Him. It is only up to us to trust Him for the next step. And because of everything Jesus has already done for us, that is not hard.

Right here—right now—will you choose to take the next step into your unknown and trust Him for His all-known? Will you purpose to carry His amazing Spirit where He wants to go?

Within this hallowed place, you will experience the glorious release of His wild presence.

ENCOUNTER HIM THROUGH *Prayer*

Lord Jesus,

I get it now—the more I heed Your voice, the more I hear Your voice, and I want to hear more. I recognize that the biggest factor in my delivering Your presence is basic obedience. It's simply trusting Your way more than my way. I understand that trusting You in my head isn't trust at all . . . if my feet do not follow.

I choose to bring to the cross every part of me that quenches the move of Your Spirit, especially my fear and pride.

Right now, Lord, I covenant with You as You place me where You want to go. May my life become like water in Your palm, rolling and repositioning into the world around me with the liquid fluidity of the Holy Spirit.

From this day forward, I choose to look intently, listen actively and do what You call me to do, so that through this vessel the world around me will experience Your love—and encounter Your wild presence.

4

Wild Patience

Whatever happens, my dear brothers and sister,
rejoice in the Lord.

Philippians 3:1

Never ask God for patience. Your whole life will fall apart!
Though spoken tongue in cheek, that saying is something I
have heard my entire life. As much as this sentiment is a joke,
it is also truth. The only way we can learn genuine patience
is to practice genuine patience. The only way we can practice
patience is if we have events in our life that require patience.

Since patience is one of the fruits of the Spirit mentioned
in Galatians 5:22, sincerely seeking it should be a worthy
pursuit—especially when we know that God is good all the
time.

God is good *all the time.*

Our circumstances and emotions have no bearing on this
truth. Our perceptions cannot unravel or fray the very nature

of our King. When our experiences rock our world in a negative way, they do not rock His. And when our focus is on His world, we will not rock either. Within this place is the forge of our God's wild patience.

In Matthew 8:23–27, Jesus and the disciples found themselves in an unexpected, savage storm. The disciples were focused on the power of the storm—and their hearts melted with fear. Jesus was focused on the power of the One who controls the storm, and His heart melted into pure peace, as evidenced by the fact that He slept through what others thought would destroy them.

The single difference between Jesus and the disciples was where their focus rested. And I have heard Pastor Bill Johnson say wisely, "You can only have authority over the storms you can sleep through."

You have this same choice. You can choose to focus on your great big problems or our great big God. Despite your words, when a challenge befalls you, your true choice will be evidenced in what your life produces: panic or peace. You can focus on yourself. Or you can focus on your Savior.

Attaining God's Wild Patience through Hardship

It was a Sunday morning in January. The thermometer outside the kitchen window had flatlined at zero. Appearing to be in no particular hurry, the last few snowflakes wafted down, seemingly oblivious to the monstrous storm that preceded them. Situated in our living room before several large windows, Troy and I were praying side by side. The view was glorious. From the elevation of our home, we could see over much of the three ranch properties. Every blade, branch and building was buried under several feet of pure white peace.

I was on my knees, arms open, palms forward, praising Jesus for the abundance of life-giving snow that had blanketed our high desert region. Together we prayed over the New Year and all that our Almighty would choose to fill it with. We prayed that His Spirit, His very presence, would cover, fill and flow through us just as the pure white snow before us consumed all in deep white folds. I started to ask that He would reveal anything in our hearts, lives or ministry that could hinder or quench the flow of His Spirit.

Suddenly, across the valley below on the west ranch, a visual vacancy appeared through the trees, followed by an explosion. A huge plume rose ominously over the shop and indoor arena.

My stunned prayer was nothing more than, *Jesus, Jesus, Jesus!*

Quickly pulling on our winter gear, Troy and I rushed down the hill to see what had happened. We arrived to discover that the entire indoor arena had collapsed violently under the weight of the snow. In a single moment, my mind raced through endless scenarios.

Was someone inside? Are they hurt? Are they pinned? Holy Spirit, help!

Going down a mental checklist, I realized that all but one of the four families who live on the west and north ranch properties were either out of town or not home.

But one family was home, and it was part of their morning routine to enter this building, load up a tractor with hay and take it out to our herd of horses. Because this indoor arena was dark and dusty, we put it to good use, storing all our ranch equipment under its expansive roof and parking our trucks, tractors, horse trailers and haying implements in neat rows.

Forsaking all logical caution, we squeezed through a buckled gap between the crumpled door and wall. Once inside, we assessed the damage, which was staggering. This previously well-organized space was unrecognizable.

Huge support beams had come down with such force that they fractured into a billion shards of splintered wood. Metal reinforcements now lay twisted under the rubble. What used to be a building was instantly reduced into utter devastation. Although the sidewalls remained relatively upright, the bulk of the snow's weight down the middle completely overwhelmed the trusses' load-bearing limits. This resulted in total failure of the entire roof with the greatest damage down the center of the structure.

Everything inside this building now lay buried under tons of debris, ice and snow. Cautiously, Troy and I slipped back out through the narrow opening in time to see Jeff and his two-year-old son, Peter, our adopted grandson, drive up on a Ranger. They were safe. In that moment, nothing else mattered.

Jeff shared how he was just leaving with Peter when his wife, Kelsie, asked if she could take a quick shower before he stepped out. Slightly frustrated over the delay, Jeff stayed inside a few moments longer to watch over their newest arrival, three-week-old Benjamin.

Upon hearing the story, I heard the Holy Spirit reveal His plan. Tears flooded my eyes at the realization of what should have happened, but did not. With a heart engulfed in gratitude, I said, "Jeff, do you understand that the Lord used your wife's shower to delay you just long enough to save your life—and the life of your son?"

Emerging recognition transformed his face into an expression that I will never forget.

We also learned that another resident on the main ranch property had come down earlier to use the small tractor to free his truck from the snow. He returned the tractor inside the arena only moments before it came crushing down.

Splintered wood and twisted metal can both be replaced; loved ones cannot.

After several trips down to the collapsed arena, Troy and I returned to our home. Stripping off all my layers of winter gear, I hung each item carefully on the hooks by the front door. I walked back into the living room and stood motionless before the great windows. Without warning, my heart was overwhelmed with the same shaky, adrenalized feeling one would have after witnessing a fatal accident, but everyone walked away unharmed.

The Holy Spirit's presence was palpable. Heaven came to earth; certain death was thwarted. The weight of this truth sent silent tears streaming down my face. This day could have turned out so differently. In this moment, I could have fallen to the floor, grieving unfathomable loss. Instead, I fell to my knees in immeasurable gratitude.

Streams of praises poured from my mouth. Arms rose in chorus with a heart overflowing with thankfulness. As if answering in a celestial call and response, rays of sunlight broke through the somber gray of the sky. Pure light streamed over pure white, creating a blinding array of what pure holiness must look like.

Igniting within my heart, His voice burned through. *Look . . . My promises are new!*

I glanced up. That is when it caught my eye. I watched it form in a perfectly vertical line. A very rare fire rainbow appeared—directly over the collapsed arena.

Defying the heavy drab sky, the fire rainbow blazed against impossible odds. Literally searing through the gray, it gained intensity for about sixty seconds. Every spectrum of the rainbow burned through the dullness. And then, as if it were a wink from the Father Himself, it vanished nearly as quickly as it formed.

Some might dismiss it as a natural phenomenon, a coincidence or another explanation that fits within the tiny confines of human logic. But this daughter of the King saw and received it as a promise sent from her Dad, wrapped in a package she would recognize.

The message was simple: *Beloved, I've got your circumstances. I've got a plan and I've got you—now is the time to trust Me!*

God is good all the time.

Once again, our circumstances and emotions have no bearing on this truth. Our perceptions cannot unravel or fray the very nature of our King. When our experiences negatively rock our world, they do not rock His. And when our focus is on His world, we will not rock either.

"Oh, give thanks to the LORD, for He is good! For his mercy endures forever" (Psalm 136:1 NKJV).

Three days later, the ranch mechanic shop—the remaining eastern portion of the same building—also collapsed. Like the arena, it came down in such a strategically safe way. No one was hurt. Once all the trusses failed on both sides of a single dividing wall, we began the process of carefully evaluating how to proceed.

Interestingly, I had prayed for God to lead us. His immediate answer was for the arena and mechanic shop to be obliterated. The truth is, we ask God to guide our lives, and He *does*—but rarely in ways we expect.

Learning to Embrace His "Mud in Our Eye" as a Precious Gift

Consider the blind man in John 9:1–15. He was born blind. Jesus did not snap His fingers so the blind man could see instantly, which is what the blind man wanted. Jesus did nearly the opposite. He spit on the ground and made mud. If that was not gross enough, He then rubbed spitty mud into eyes that were already blind.

Jesus, what? How was that helping? Are You serious, Lord? How can this be Your answer?

And if that was not enough insult to a blind man, Jesus then told him to go wash his face in a pool that was far away. The man is still blind. And now he has the extra burden of a face full of spitty mud.

So this is God's answer? Are you kidding me?

Many times, when we cry out to God for help, what we get in return is mud in our eye. Let me explain

Often, when we ask God for assistance, it appears as if the opposite happens. Something catastrophic occurs, and we turn to God immediately and plead for His intervention. Frequently, what we receive looks more like even greater destruction to our situation. From our limited perspective, when our prayers are not answered in the way we expect, we assume that God has not answered our prayers and, therefore, has abandoned us. We believe that He is somehow not paying attention to our pain. Because we perceive Him as having a lackadaisical attitude in our time of need, we presume that He does not really love us.

Unfortunately, for many this is where the journey of trust in God ends.

When we lack the endurance we need to wait on God's timing, we fail to trust Him long enough to realize that this is exactly where the wild patience of our God begins.

When God's response does not fit into our understanding, it is easy to spiral into a place of frustration and loneliness. We ask our Lord for help, and our immediate situation gets worse. Our prayers are not answered quickly, so we somehow believe we cannot trust God and now need to answer our own prayer.

Case in point: Jesus all but spit in the blind man's face and sent him away still blind. It is pretty safe to speculate that this was *not* the answer the blind man wanted.

But it was the answer Jesus gave.

When I asked God to reveal our weaknesses, the immediate answer was not what I expected. I could not fathom that His answer would be our arena and mechanic shop—and beneath it every tool and ranch implement we owned—being crushed.

God, what? How is this Your best?

In that moment, it would have been easy to sink into a place where His response felt more like spitty mud in my eyes.

In the aftermath, Troy and I took on the task of documenting photographically all the pulverized equipment inside. Carefully maneuvering through the devastation, the Holy Spirit opened my eyes to see something astonishing.

This building was 168 feet long and 72 feet wide. It had 14 trusses, each being about 12 inches wide and spaced 12 feet apart. When these massive structures collapsed over our four trucks, three horse trailers, two tractors, a CAT, hay rake, hay baler, bale wagon, hay mower, manure spreader, flatbed trailer and various other ranch implements, they crushed down between each one. Miraculously, over twenty pieces of heavy equipment—parked at "random"—were each located *exactly* between the devastating force of every single truss. One truck was so narrowly missed that the side-view mirrors were sliced off. But the truck itself sustained only a few minor dings. Of all the ranch's rolling fleet, only one steel stock trailer was hit by a truss. The beam was deflected by the hayrack, and the trailer sustained no damage—not one single dent.

In John 9:1–15, the blind man took one unseeing step after another, connecting each step of faith to another. Each step drew him closer to something yet undefined. Each step strengthened his faith for what was coming. Each step confirmed within his own heart that he undeniably believed Jesus. We know this because he kept walking. He took action; he did what Jesus asked him to do—despite how completely ridiculous it must have seemed at the time. He kept taking the next step of faith.

In verse 7, we find Jesus telling the blind man, "Go wash yourself in the pool of Siloam" (*Siloam* means "sent"). So the man went and washed, and then came back seeing.

Forging God's Wild Patience through Our Blind Faith Walk

Patience in Christ is forged in what I call the blind faith walk. Each consecutive step builds upon the strength of the last, drawing us closer to the pool where restoration resides. Faith, trust, perseverance and patience can only be refined when we have unique opportunities that allow them to be put to the test.

It would not be a faith walk if we could see.

When we take steps into our unknown, our impossible, we usher in a genuine experience of His *all*-known, His always possible.

About Jesus, the blind man said, "He put the mud over my eyes, and when I washed it away, I could see!" (John 9:15). Later he said, "Yes, Lord, I believe!" and worshiped Him (v. 38).

No matter what God's answer might be to your immediate prayers for help, do not despair or waver from trusting Him. Regardless of how devastating, confusing or bleak His momentary response might seem, you can believe in Him for the outcome. Today, choose to answer, *Yes, Lord, I believe!* and worship Jesus.

The apostle Paul wrote,

> I have learned to be content with whatever I have. I know how to live on almost nothing or with everything. I have learned the secret of living in every situation, whether it is with a full stomach or empty, with plenty or little. For I can do everything through Christ, who gives me strength.
>
> Philippians 4:11–13

Whatever your previous plans might have been, God's plans are always *better*. Choose to trust Him through the blind faith walk. Only then will you stride beyond your "good" and into His "better" . . . which is always His very *best*.

In John's gospel, the blind man exemplifies what Jesus desires from each of us when we call on His name—obedient trust. The blind man did not question, complain or quit. He did *exactly* what Jesus asked him to do. And that is when the fullness of his request was fulfilled.

Mary and Martha are another example of mud in the eyes. They sent word to Jesus, asking Him to hurry to them and heal their brother. Jesus did not hurry. He did the opposite; He chose to stay where He was for a few more days. Jesus waited until the situation got as bad as it could get—Lazarus died. How is that an answer to prayer? But it was.

"So he told them plainly, 'Lazarus is dead. And for your sakes, I'm glad I wasn't there, for now you will *really believe*. Come, let's go see him'" (John 11:14–15, emphasis added).

Jesus Himself asked the same question that we often do: "Should I pray, 'Father, save me from this hour'? But this is the very reason I came! Father, bring glory to your name" (John 12:27–28).

Often, learning the wild patience of our God begins with a blind faith walk—something that seems utterly impossible.

But "with God everything is possible" (Matthew 19:26). We know this truth, yet rarely do we actually believe it. But the more we believe it, the more we see Him work in crazy, amazing ways around us.

The truth is, no matter what we face, there is *always* a way through; there is always a faith walk. This seemingly unattainable path will lead us to the exact limits of our trust—and if we keep walking, it leads straight through the furnace where trust is refined into faith. From this flame, we step directly into the very presence of God.

Troy and I prayed for clarity—and instantly the biggest building our ministry had collapsed with everything we owned inside. The blind man asked to see—and he received mud smeared into his eyes and was sent away . . . still blind. Mary and Martha pleaded for their brother to be healed—and Jesus waited until their brother died. Even Jesus asked God the Father to remove His cup of impending suffering—and He went to the cross.

So where was God? Right where He has always been: still on the throne, still leading those who seek Him into His perfect plan.

Are you seeing the pattern? We ask God for help in circumstances, and instead of taking us out of them, He sends us on a blind faith walk straight through them.

The blind man's faith walk led him directly toward what he wanted most—sight and greater belief in God. Mary, Martha

71

and Lazarus' faith walk led them directly toward what they wanted most—complete healing and greater belief in God. Jesus' faith walk led Him directly toward what He wanted most—taking back the keys to sin and death and making a way for even greater belief in God.

Had any of them crossed their arms over their chest and refused the blind faith walk, none would have ever experienced what they sought most deeply.

When we reject God's plan because it appears impossible, that is where we end up living—in the self-made prison of human impossibilities. But when we choose to trust God beyond our human realm of impossible, we experience the fullness of faith that His "possible" is designed to forge within us.

"Be thankful in all circumstances, for this is God's will for you who belong to Christ Jesus" (1 Thessalonians 5:18).

When we asked God to show us weakness in our ministry—and our indoor arena and mechanic shop came down—it was a $500,000 loss. Not quite the answer we had in mind. But as we journeyed through our own blind faith walk, His greater purpose started to come into focus. Clearly, all the people were spared, and all the contents were spared. All we lost was the structure.

Soon, our question began to sound like, *Lord, it appears that You did not want this building, so what do You want?*

His answer was nearly as immediate as the building collapse: *I want a pasture for My sheep. It will look like a park for My people.*

Right next to our Big Barn Fellowship Hall, a picture started to swirl in my mind. A grassy amphitheater would be surrounded by shade trees. The area beyond the trees where the old indoor arena once stood would be covered in grass and gardens. It would hold a pavilion with barnwood tables and a massive fire pit. Beyond that would be an area for playing volleyball, cornhole and horseshoes, as well as a swing set. Over on top of the remaining concrete slab would stand a basketball and four-square court. And nearly every inch of concrete would be lovingly covered with children's drawings in colored chalk. Where a dusty old dark building once stood, a park would arise that would beckon an entire community to come together and hear the Gospel of the King.

Friend, seeking patience is a worthy pursuit. Say yes to His blind faith walk. Believe that He will meet you in the journey. Worship Him every step of the way. This is the beautiful path that leads to the wild patience of our God.

Let's choose together to "give thanks unto the LORD, for he is good!" (Psalm 107:1). No matter what challenges you might face, this message stands true for all—*God is good.* We can trust Him within any blind faith walk.

"May the Lord lead your hearts into a full understanding and expression of the love of God and the patient endurance that comes from Christ" (2 Thessalonians 3:5).

ENCOUNTER HIM THROUGH *Prayer*

King Jesus,

I acknowledge that "Yeah, but . . ." is a phrase that only exists on my side of heaven. Today, I choose to lay this crutch of faithlessness at Your feet—no more excuses. When Your answers look vastly different from what I've asked for, may my response be nothing less than praise and gratitude.

I choose You over my comfort.

Lord, when the journey doesn't make sense, I will stand on the truth that You always provide a way through. Your faith walk will lead me to the limits of my trust—and if I keep walking, I'll move straight through this fiery furnace place and directly into Your arms.

Holy Spirit, patience is a fruit of Your presence. I want You to smear Your mud over my eyes! I want to walk this life trusting only in You. I want to wash in Your pool of faith and see You and Your plan with sharp clarity.

Jesus, please draw me through that sacred ring of suffering. I want to live the rest of my days in that place where I, too, can look up into Your beautiful face and declare, "Yes, Lord, I believe!" and fall before You in worship.

Lord, You see my heart, and You know I don't really want to suffer, but I really do want You. Because hardship unites me with You, today I ask for Your wild patience.

PART TWO

Encountering Adoration of Him

5

Wild Praise

All the earth bows down to you; they sing praise
to you, they sing the praises of your name.

Psalm 66:4 NIV

The wild praise of our God is reflected all around us.

Every heart of flesh was created with the capacity to know
God (see Romans 1:19–20), to see Him through His creation.
The more we observe His artwork, the more we learn about
the beautiful, powerful, pure, complex nature of our wild God.

It is interesting how His praise is reflected everywhere
within nature (see Psalm 145:10), but seldom within the
hearts of men. Perhaps if we emulated the wilderness more,
we would experience more of the wild praise of the One
who made it.

For this girl's heart, few things reflect the glorious facets
of God more than a downy layer of untouched snow.

Trusting God for the Beautiful Result of Our Burdens

Not long ago, on a cold morning in late winter, I went to my office to pray. This devotional time with my Lord comes first—always before my day begins. While cradling a hot cup of coffee to warm my hands, I settled into my chair and surveyed the darkened world beyond my window. It was early, and the first rays of sunlight had yet to break over the top of the butte upon which I live. A heavy snow had fallen during the night, mantling all creation beneath a perfect cloak of frozen white. As if asleep, this faultless world lay completely motionless.

Scanning the small vista, my meandering gaze rested on a single vignette.

Swathed within a flawless cone of snow stood a solitary twelve-foot pine tree. Its symmetrical form appeared to be bent low by the weight it bore. Each bough hung heavy, curving downward toward the earth, yielding its strength to the encumbering load. As I considered the burdened conifer, its general appearance looked . . . *sad*. Its normally uplifted profile appeared completely diminished. Each of its needled arms were cast low, weighted down by the onus they bore. Framed within the gray light of dawn, the tree mirrored silently what sorrow might look like.

Continuing to observe this bent soldier, I felt a slow draw, an odd connection. Rising through the stillness, a realization dawned: I could relate to how this tree looked. Occasionally, I experience a similar sense of being laden with the arduous weight of concerns this life can blizzard down.

Lord, I prayed, *there are rare times when I do feel just like that tree. Sometimes I do feel bent beneath the overwhelming load of the things I'm called to bear. At times, I can feel crushed under a great burden of heaviness.*

Through the dim light, I heard within my heart His unmistakable voice.

I know, Beloved.

In the utter stillness that followed, His gentle voice continued, *As My creation reflects, will you also trust Me through your seasons of burden?*

I found myself nodding in agreement. The answer within my heart was not audible. *Yes. Jesus, I will choose to trust You.*

The stillness gave way to a sudden transformation. Everything changed. Instantly, a laser shaft of pure light pierced the dim beginning of dawn—the sun was rising.

As the sun's brilliance overtook the crest of the butte where my home rests, its glory came rushing down. In a simultaneous wave, pure golden rays of redeeming light poured through creation. Flowing like a healing river, revitalizing beams streamed down the hill, through the lonely tree, into my office and across my cheeks.

Nearly startled by the visual explosion of dawn, I sat in complete wonder, mesmerized by what unfolded next.

Instantaneously, the burdened tree, now drenched in flooding light, no longer looked sad at all. On the contrary, instead of appearing subdued and forlorn, something extraordinary began to transpire. Softly, slowly, the tree started to radiate. It appeared to revel in its intrinsic ability to reflect the rising brilliance that shone around it. As the sun continued its eternally unchallenged ascension, the yoke of burden upon the tree shifted. Completely powerless against the ensuing warmth, the white encumbrance began to glisten.

The snow was melting. What, only minutes prior, looked frozen and despondent was now beginning to shimmer with a countless array of fiery droplets. Resulting from the burden itself, each bead of water sparkled with the prismatic radiance of the sun. Hanging heavier by the moment, they danced in their own exhibition of light. Bending pure white radiance, each drop blazed in flashes of intense blue, violet, orange, green, yellow and red.

Then it happened. The first droplet fell. As if heralding a chorus to arise in one life-giving accord, an incandescent rain began to fall beneath the once-grieving tree.

The burden itself was falling away—in its wake, life was being renewed to the tree's foundation.

Caught up in the cheering refrain, a single bough released its saturated load and bounced skyward. By its very action, it seemed to beckon its comrades to come join in the new freedom. As if called to muster, a domino effect poured over the entire tree in a single moment. In near unison, virtually every branch laid its burdens down in a flurried avalanche of white liberation. Bough after bough sprang up with a silent shout, stretching, waving, reaching up toward the heavens in a conifer's song of praise to its King.

"Jesus!" was the only word I could utter. The glory of the moment was followed by truth—His truth.

Indeed, Beloved, you are just like this tree. You can also make the decision to praise Me through any storm, from beneath any burden. When you choose what seems impossible— to worship Me through your darkness—something powerful happens. The chains imprisoning your hope, your joy, your love loose their grip and fall away. In the wake of your choice to praise Me will grow a stronger hope, a greater joy, a deeper love. Because of your chosen response to not only trust Me but actually praise Me through your burden, My freedom will be released over and through you.

Indeed, you are like the tree: you, too, can choose to lay your burdens down and lift your arms to Me. From this place of gratitude, joy—My joy—is cultivated within your heart.

Understanding poured into my soul as the intense light poured into my office. I can praise my King through *anything*. Because He has given me this choice, there is *no* burden in this life that can imprison or steal what He gives so freely.

The little tree showed me that choosing to praise God beneath my heavy load is exactly like hailing the sun to rise. Our God inhabits the praises of His people (Psalm 22:3). He Himself beams His healing glory into our hearts the instant we choose to still believe in Him and trust in Him, not bowing beneath the weight of troubles that befall us. The Spirit of the living God fills our praise and exchanges our pain for His joy.

"Let us offer through Jesus a *continual sacrifice of praise to God*, proclaiming our allegiance to his name" (Hebrews 13:15, emphasis added).

From Pit to Palace by Way of Praise

A very personal awakening occurs the moment we understand that we can choose to praise Jesus through any darkness that might befall us. Doing so does not mean that our troubling circumstances will go away; it means that the prison of heaviness we feel *because* of them will.

God does not promise that we will never know another storm. He promises that—if we choose to praise Him—He will come to us in the midst of every single one. He promises that He, the Lord of all, will personally inhabit our praise.

God with us. What storm in this life is not worth that?

81

The blizzards will come. They will mantle our heart with a frozen layer of anger, sorrow, fear, grief, uncertainty and unforgiveness. We will feel the penetrating bitterness that can make our very bones ache. But, friend, please understand: this is a place to travel through, not a place to camp out and live.

When we choose to build a home in our pain, we give up our birthright of joy—a birthright Jesus Christ secured for each of us by giving His life. Instead of walking through the "valley of the shadow of death" (Psalm 23:4 KJV) with Him, many quit in the middle—and blame Him. Many believers have chosen to live in this darkened place for so long that they believe cold and gray is normal. Left in this place, the icy weight of all that encumbers them crushes their hearts slowly until they suffocate from a lack of truth. Satan wishes for all our stories to end that way: through death beneath the weight of our heavy hearts. Indeed, for many believers, this is their self-appointed end.

But it does not have to be.

Jesus did not die on the cross so we could stay imprisoned in oppression.

He gives all of us a way to break free from the crushing yoke of sorrow. When we are bent by our burdens, frozen to the earth in complete immobility, we might resemble the heavily laden tree. From the outside we look motionless, hopeless, lifeless. But God's wild praise is not quenched by our circumstances. It cannot be subdued, because it is not conjured from beyond our life but from inside it.

Deep within our hearts is a sacred place, a hallowed furnace that longs to be set ablaze by His holy fire. True ignition happens when we choose gratitude in Him over grief in our circumstances. Within this holy flame, our pain melts before the glory of His presence and is remade—forged into white-hot joy.

Sound too fantastic to be real? Indeed, from a human perspective it is. But God does not call us to view this world from the ground level. He calls us to trust His perspective from His level.

Paul and Silas exemplified this perfectly in Acts 16. They were doing exactly what the Holy Spirit had instructed—preaching the Gospel. Suddenly, they were falsely accused, stripped naked in public and beaten almost to death. If that were not bad enough, they were then thrown into the deepest, darkest dungeon in the land, and then their ankles were locked into stocks.

They did nothing wrong. They were doing everything the Holy Spirit had asked them to do. From the ground level, no one would have blamed them for parking in the middle of the "valley of the shadow of death" (Psalm 23:4 KJV) and cursing God, but they chose not to. Why? Because they were not viewing their circumstances from the ground level; they were literally under the ground level. Instead, they chose to ignite the holy fire, to praise God in their pain. Sitting in the darkness in a pool of their own blood and filth, they chose joy and sang praises to God.

We all know the result. The Holy Spirit came and filled their praise. He inhabited them. His presence shook the prison, and all the doors swung open. All the prisoners got saved. The jailer got saved. The jailer's entire family got saved—everyone turned to the saving hope of Jesus. Why? Because when we choose joy in our hardships, Jesus chooses to crush our hardships with joy. The Holy Spirit comes in, and the entire atmosphere transforms in the presence of His glory.

The deepest, blackest dungeon could not contain Paul and Silas' joy. It was their praise amid pain that beckoned the Holy Spirit to fill that dark, stench-filled cavern with the glory of God.

Choosing joy can transform any pit into a palace.

When imprisoned by adversity, we can choose to praise and worship our God. When we do, like Paul and Silas, we release the holy fire within us to surge into an inferno of white-hot freedom. The pure heat generated from a heart fueled by joyful praise knows no boundary.

Our frozen confinement crackles with tiny fractures as it succumbs to the burning passion of our choice to adore instead of curse our God. No darkness can contain genuine praise of the one true God. Like the rising of the sun, glorious beams of joy burn through evil's attempt to enslave us. In an explosion of pure light, remnants of icy heartache rain down around us as we kneel, lifting our arms—like the tree—to give glory to God.

When we dwell on God's provision, His promises, His presence, authentic joy is the natural overflow, which inspires us to praise and worship Him through our hardships. In so doing, we can experience His peace through any circumstance.

"Always be full of joy in the Lord. I say it again—rejoice!" (Philippians 4:4).

The enemy has no defense against the powerful freedom we find in the wild praise of our God. Indeed, joy in the Lord is our strength (see Nehemiah 8:10). Against this powerful freedom, the enemy cannot fight.

"Praise the Lord! For he has heard my cry for mercy. The Lord is my strength and shield. I trust him with all my heart. He helps me, and *my heart is filled with joy*. I burst out in songs of thanksgiving" (Psalm 28:6–7, emphasis added).

On this day, may we purpose to be like the little tree, bursting through every confinement to raise our arms in praise to our God. Let's live from the bedrock of filling our hearts with His uncontainable, untamable, wild praise.

"Let all that I am praise the LORD; with my whole heart, I will praise his holy name. Let all that I am praise the LORD; may I never forget the good things he does for me" (Psalm 103:1–2).

ENCOUNTER HIM THROUGH *Prayer*

Lord Jesus,

You didn't create me to continually live in a dark, painful place. I was created to live within Your brilliant light. If I find myself paralyzed in a frozen realm, I acknowledge that it's only because I've been believing a lie.

I wasn't designed to live trapped within a frozen layer of darkness—I was designed to live transformed within a glorious layer of Your presence. This is who I am in You. This is what's true.

I acknowledge that Your Word is unchanging. It instructs that when I choose joy in You—over my pain— the enemy's dark, frozen swathe melts before the consuming fire that is You. What was sent to diminish and destroy is transformed into the very thing that gives continual life. By simply choosing Your joy, I allow You to transform my painful past into present strength!

When I choose to raise my hands in praise to You, against such a weapon, the enemy has no defense. Jesus, right now, I choose joy in You. In doing so, I welcome Your white-hot surge of renewed strength to transform my heart and radiate through my uplifted hands. As Your strength fills me, I can feel the weightiness of oppression literally melting, raining off in the presence of Your glory.

Lord, praising You is a choice, and I choose to become a vessel that never stops extolling Your wild praise.

6

Wild Worship

Day after day and night after night they keep on saying, "Holy, holy, holy is the Lord God, the Almighty—the one who always was, who is, and who is still to come."

Revelation 4:8

Our Lord is worthy of our worship.

He alone is God. He is surrounded by a heavenly realm that worships Him constantly. He spoke all creation into being, and all creation responds in adoration of its Creator. If the entirety of heaven's host and all creation revere Him continually, what is stopping us from doing the same? Why are we not living in constant, focused adoration of the One we call God?

At home and throughout my travels, I have the opportunity to speak and pray with countless individuals who are engaged in mighty struggles. Almost daily, I hear a familiar plea: "My life is hopeless, my situation is hopeless, *I'm* hopeless. All is lost, there's nothing left within my circumstances but pain and despair."

The fact is—outside of Jesus Christ—all of these statements about hopelessness are true.

Yet Romans 15:13 rings equally true: "I pray that God, the source of hope, will fill you completely with joy and peace because you trust in him. Then you will overflow with confident hope through the power of the Holy Spirit."

God is our source of hope.

He desires to fill us to overflowing with hope. He offers His hope to everyone every minute of every day. So why do we choose to linger in hopelessness? The answer is simple: because our focus remains in the wrong place. Our focus is genuinely not on Him but on ourselves, and the rotten fruit of negativity is our proof.

This made me ponder the power of Jeremiah 29:11–14:

> "For I know the plans I have for you," says the LORD. "They are plans for good and not for disaster, to give you a future and a hope. In those days when you pray, I will listen. If you look for me wholeheartedly, you will find me. I will be found by you," says the LORD.

This single passage is nearly the definition of genuine hope. Most believers know this verse well and quote it often. Yet few live their lives in a manner that proves they believe it.

If I already know the Lord God Almighty has plans for my life and they are good, then why is much of my prayer directed as if to "remind" Him of that fact? If He has already promised good things to come, why do I ask Him for more? He is God. I am not. He knows the way. I do not. As a matter of fact, He is the way (see John 14:6).

Since He knows the way and is the way, instead of being a backseat driver and reminding Him of every curve, pothole and wreck ahead, what if I just rested in His presence and thanked Him for driving me—period?

What if I dedicated time in prayer—without asking Him for anything?

Would it bless God if I set special time aside to come to Him with no agenda, only to thank Him, praise Him and worship Him?

What if I came to Him with my mouth shut, with my ears wide open, and simply listened to Him and then followed His lead?

Thankful Worship: The Doorway to His Undeniable Peace

I was raised to pray in a more conventional manner. The steadfast "ask that all broken things would be restored" method has been the foundation of my prayers. Although this is not a wrong way to pray, if this is the only way we pray, it is incomplete.

Philippians 4:6–7 (emphasis added) states,

> Don't worry about anything; instead, pray about everything. Tell God what you need, and *thank him for all he has done.* Then you will experience God's peace, which exceeds anything we can understand. His peace will guard your hearts and minds as you live in Christ Jesus.

Let's thank God for all He has done. If we do this, we will experience His peace. Simply by thanking Him, He gives us peace. Living in His peace instead of our turmoil is what we desire, right?

The concept of purposely coming before the Lord in prayer—and asking for nothing and only worshiping Him— was intriguing to me. Quite some time ago, in obedience to the Holy Spirit's leading, I added this type of worship to my prayer. Since then, nothing about my life has ever been the same.

Even though Troy was on the East Coast, February 5 was the evening we chose to introduce this type of prayerful worship to our staff. All who wanted to join in for the last thirty minutes of the day were encouraged to gather in the upper room of our barn. While welcoming our beloved staff as they entered, I was also aware of a strangely powerful storm blowing in.

Our instructions were basic: Follow the leading of the Holy Spirit and allow your body to bend into a position of worship. When our body assumes a posture of worship, our heart and mind will quickly follow. If He moves you to kneel, stand, raise your arms, dance or put your forehead on the floor, do what He asks you to do. This is a time of focused worship, adoration and praise. Please do not ask Him for anything—unless *He* directs you to pray for something specific. Then, once you have finished praying as He has asked, return to a place of pure worship.

With our meager instructions in place, we dimmed the lights and turned on a thirty-minute set of worship music. As the wind roared outside, the Holy Spirit roared inside. Twice, the whole upper room of the barn shook before the mighty winds that beset it. I could not help but wonder if this was what the disciples heard and felt as they waited together for the Holy Spirit to come (see Acts 2). Sensing His presence, I felt Him "agree" heartily. He wanted me to fervently pray for the same move of the Spirit.

Following God's leading, I went facedown on the floor, then implored Him for a new release, a torrent of His presence, to wash away anything within us that might quench His flow. I asked Him to come shake our very foundation, to blow away all human distractions with His mighty breath. I pleaded with Him to send His holy fire to burn through all our hearts and purify us for His service.

Completing what I believed He had asked, I returned to worshiping the One who has redeemed my soul.

Our time of worship together finished nearly as quickly as it started. Soon, all were heading home to join their families. A dear friend stayed late. While cradling hot mugs of tea, we spoke deep into the night of the mighty things our Lord was doing. Finally, at midnight, it was time for bed.

By then, the windstorm had reached its full force. For the first time in 24 years of living in my simple home, I felt it shudder and jolt before the gale. I could hear the panes of glass crackling as they bowed and flexed with each howling blast.

At 1:00 a.m. the power went down. At 3:00 a.m. the relentless clanging of sheet metal proclaimed through the torrent that a roof somewhere below was being torn off. Throughout the night, I heard mighty trees crack and pop as ancient limbs and roots gave way. All night long the house was pummeled by a continuous siege of flying debris. Through it all, I lay alone in my bed, pondering the complete wonder of the mighty power and authority of our God. During the sleepless hours, I had no fear, only awe. This girl's heart praised her heavenly Father for answering earlier prayer in such an unmistakable way.

Alone in the darkness, surrounded by the storm, I was profoundly aware of something unmistakable—God's pleasure.

Dawn broke to what felt like a whole new world. Indeed, this was an epic storm. Locally, a single gust of wind was clocked at 118 miles per hour. Throughout the morning, it was clear within my travels to the three nearby towns that all had sustained damage, but our small community of Tumalo was annihilated. One could see where microbursts of wind had hit the ground and traveled great distances, flattening everything in their path.

Over the course of the day, I noticed something unusual. Our ranch lies at the center of a triangle of towns. We are close to equal distances from each one. Yet somehow, swathes of microburst destruction lay in lines upon the earth that pointed toward the ranch. One started approximately three miles away, hitting multiple properties and leveling barns, storage sheds, fences, gates and trees. It led to the base of the butte upon which we live. It crashed down trees in strips as it skipped up one side and down the other directly toward our barn.

I inspected the ranch under gray skies that were still tossed by the wind. Our property lost seven large trees, one of which fell on our mercantile, completely crushing the awning. Various building materials and debris were scattered everywhere. Outhouses were lifted and tossed over a fence. One of our metal wheel lines was completely torn in two. The untethered half was blown over one hundred yards across our hay field.

Amid all the damage, however, what intrigued me most was the blown-off roof that was currently relocated upside down in our arena. Of the multitude of roofs that dot the ranch, the only one to blow off was the one that covered the *exact* area we had been praying beneath the night before.

I could not help but wonder what the Lord was trying to show me.

The answer came the next morning.

I awoke to absolute calm. Even while getting dressed, I could sense something distinctive in the air. There was a loving thrill, a parental draw, a grinning beckon from the Father.

Come, Beloved. Walk with Me.

I pulled on my boots quickly and stepped out into the cold dawn. It took only a few steps across our deck before my eyes locked onto what He wanted me to see. I could feel myself blinking hard, as if my eyes themselves were testing what filled them. In pure awe, I heard His name fall out of my mouth: "Jesus!" The sight that greeted me made my knees weak. It was unmistakable. The Lord spoke in a language I understand, the undeniable voice of creation itself.

Arcing before me in living color was a rainbow—but not just any rainbow. This blaze of iridized splendor streamed out of heaven, not near, beyond or behind but *into* the gaping hole torn through the barn roof. Its glory could be seen pouring into and filling the room.

Human words fail to capture or describe this glorious covenant that only God could create. His everlasting symbol of promise was burning down into the room where we had purposed to engage in immersion worship of Him. The King of all was showing me His pleasure, His favor, His approval of anyone seeking Him in pure-hearted worship. Jesus said,

"But the time is coming—indeed it's here now—when true worshipers will worship the Father in spirit and in truth. The Father is looking for those who will worship him that way. For God is Spirit, so those who worship him must worship in spirit and in truth."

John 4:23–24

In Spirit and in truth. God desires us to come to Him with *all* that we are—heart, soul, mind and strength—and worship *all* that He is.

Releasing the Spirit's Power and Intention through Worship

When we worship God in Spirit and in truth, His Spirit is released into the atmosphere around us. Through worship, the Holy Spirit transforms our environment—in any way He pleases—to give God glory. True worship releases the miraculous power of God.

God's Word is filled with examples of this beautiful phenomenon. When we choose to worship God in the face of challenge, everything changes because we change—our heart realigns before the truth of who He is.

Elijah worshiped God, and his foes were exposed and defeated (see 1 Kings 18). According to most of the psalms, King David's love and worship of God transformed him into a man after God's own heart (see also Acts 13:22). Daniel worshiped God, and the mouths of hungry lions were closed (see Daniel 6:1–23). Daniel's friends Hananiah, Mishael and Azariah (Shadrach, Meshach and Abednego) worshiped God and were thrown into a fiery inferno. Not only did the furnace have no effect on them, but Jesus Himself met them there (see Daniel 3). Simeon the priest was a worshiper of God and got to see and hold the Messiah (see Luke 2:28–32). Peter worshiped God and saw a new freedom revealed from heaven (see Acts 10). Lydia was a worshiper of God, and she and her household were redeemed (see Acts 16:13–15). Paul and Silas worshiped God, and prison doors were opened and all present received salvation (see Acts 16:16–34). John was a worshiper of God and was taken into the heavenly realms (see Revelation 1:9–18).

Pure-hearted worship releases the power and intention of the Holy Spirit. The more we worship Him through everything, the more everything is transformed in us and around us by His presence.

Indeed, God is worthy of our worship, but He does not need it—He is God. Instead, like any loving father, His desire for us is to desire Him. He appeals to those who call Him Lord to willingly, continually affirm and reaffirm our heart after His. What dad does not want his child to frequently seek his presence for no other reason than to say, "I love you, Daddy"? Such pure adoration rises into the heavenly realms like sweet perfume before Him. He delights in this genuine gift lifted from the hearts of His people.

"The LORD's delight is in those who fear him, those who put their hope in his unfailing love" (Psalm 147:11).

I can choose to honor Him no matter what tempest I face. Experiencing the storm and the rainbow remind me that when it comes to hopelessness, I have a choice to make. We each have a choice to make.

When we choose to focus on the storm, our despair and fear grow, and our trust in Jesus shrinks. Out of habit, we pray from our position of absolute need—because our focus is on our need more than our Savior.

Or, we can choose to come to our Lord within our personal storms and worship Him because He still redeems, He still loves and He is still God. The truth is, no storm of dark circumstances can contain the peace that fills us when we turn to Him in pure worship (Philippians 4:7).

Our willing adoration of God is a weapon of spiritual warfare against which our enemy has no defense.

"Come, let us worship and bow down. Let us kneel before the LORD our maker, for he is our God" (Psalm 95:6–7).

The more we know Jesus, really know Him—what He has done and who He is—the more our understanding of genuine hope will overshadow and eventually consume all our fears. Worship fuels this process, and that is a choice worth making.

ENCOUNTER HIM THROUGH *Prayer*

Lord Jesus,

You inhabit, You come into, You live within the praise and worship of Your people. This single fact should be enough to instantly draw me into worshiping You no matter what I face. And yet often my focus remains stuck on all that still hurts.

Savior, this is where I come to the beautiful Y in the road—I can remain stuck with my focus on me, or I can reposition my focus on You because You're still God and You're still worthy of my worship.

When I engage You in worship through my heartaches and hardships, Your presence fills me and overflows into the atmosphere around me. It's Your presence that overshadows and consumes every fear.

Jesus, my simple worship of You releases the power and intention of the Holy Spirit. The more I worship You through everything, the more Your presence transforms everything around me.

Lord, worship is one of the mighty weapons of war in which the enemy has no power against us—none. Your Word is clear that my worship invites a spiritual annihilation that the enemy is terrified of. He's terrified of You in me, not the other way around. Jesus, help me get my head around this truth and stand up in Your presence and fight back.

In this moment, I choose to wage war in the spiritual realm by consistently engaging You in immersion worship. Jesus, reveal the days and times You desire for me to weekly kneel before You in complete submission and adoration. Right now, I choose to make room to seek Your face. I will ask for nothing—I come only to praise and worship You.

May my pure adoration become the clarion call for Your very presence to extend and inhabit the place within me that only You can. Come, wild Spirit, come and fill my worship now.

7

Wild Giving

Three things will last forever—faith, hope, and love—and the greatest of these is love.

1 Corinthians 13:13

Our God is the wildest Giver of all.

His giving is lavish and simple. It is powerful and peaceful. It is extreme and detailed. Every gift He gives changes us on a foundational level—that is good giving.

The older I get, the more I realize that a "true gift" is rarely something that can be purchased. It is usually a token or action given to symbolize one heart arcing to another. This kind of gift rises out of a place outside the reach of worldly finances; it is different from what money can buy. The value of a true gift is priceless.

Defeating Pain with the Unstoppable Gift of Jesus' Love

"Get away from me!" the boy shouted and then turned and kicked the indoor arena wall.

I was speaking at a university and, between engagements, had been invited to assist in a special session with high-risk kids. I had been warned that the boy I would be working with was extremely volatile and had broken bones in his therapist's face and torso.

Understandably, his therapist's expression was one of exhaustion and defeat. "He's all yours," she said after the pre-teen screamed at both of us to leave him alone.

I took a few indirect steps toward him. "What's your name?" I asked in a quiet, nonchalant tone.

His response was a menacing growl. He covered his face with his hands, which, from his perspective, made me go away. His pudgy body gave silent witness that food was very important to him, clearly his primary method of comfort and refuge.

My thoughts turned to the only One who truly knew this broken little boy. *Jesus, how do I reach him? How do I get beneath his anger to his pain, to the place only You can heal? Lord, You're the only One who knows. Lead me, Holy Spirit.*

Sensing that I needed to be less intimidating, less adultlike, I leaned against the wall near the boy and quietly slid down into a crouching position. Three horses had been released at random into the arena. Two moved together, the third stood alone. Following the Holy Spirit, I began to softly speak.

"See that horse over there? She's all by herself. You can tell by the way she's standing that she's really sad."

No response.

So I continued to narrate what I saw. "She doesn't want to be alone, but she's afraid of a lot of stuff. She's afraid of being rejected and abandoned . . . again." I stole a glance at my young friend and saw his hands slowly drop away from his eyes only.

Without acknowledging me, he turned slightly to look at the mare over the tips of his fingers. As his hands dropped and hung suspended in front of his chest, I studied him. He had sandy hair and dark blue eyes. His facial expression seemed to slowly melt from rage to sorrow, mirroring the same pain that the solitary mare bore. He stared at her intently.

Breaking the silence, I said, "I've felt that way too. It's no fun. I don't want her to hurt anymore. I'm gonna go talk to her. Wanna come?"

Again, without looking at me, the boy nodded in wordless agreement.

Walking toward the sad mare, I said, "My name's Kim. What's yours?"

Again, without eye contact, he muttered, "Nathan."

"Thanks, Nathan, for helping me. I think it's gonna take both of us to help move her out of her loneliness and pain. She doesn't realize it yet, but the truth is, she doesn't have to stay in that sad place ever again."

No response.

As we closed the distance to the mare, she took a few steps away from us. "See that? She's avoiding us. She'd rather be alone than be rejected again. What do ya think we should do about that?"

He shrugged his shoulders in the universal "don't know, don't care" gesture.

"Hey, let's prove her wrong!" I encouraged. Then I stepped in front of the chestnut-and-white-painted mare and blocked her evasion.

As if by rote, she stopped. Her years of handling had trained her to be obedient, nothing more. She was old. Her hollowed body and stiff joints testified to that fact. Her eyes were dull and lifeless, focused on nothing.

Gently, I reached out and cupped her jaw. No response. She, too, had retreated deep inside herself.

Again, I narrated my observations to Nathan. "She's in there . . . somewhere. We just have to coax her to come out. How do you think we should do that?"

Again, he shrugged his shoulders in wordless indifference.

"When I was in a dark place, what finally made me come out of my pain . . . was love. I think she needs to know that we love her. We can stand here and tell her that all day long, but real love goes beyond words. Real love is expressed in actions."

I watched Nathan. His dark eyes were fixed on the sad horse. His lips parted in deep thought. Slowly and without instruction, he placed the palm of his hand on her side.

I moved next to him and mirrored his action. Then, I added my other hand and started to rub the mare in soft circles. In what appeared to be a subconscious game, Nathan did the exact same thing.

Gradually, we moved our hands over her entire side. Her head lowered as she rested in our presence. Then I asked, "Hey, what do you think if we gave her a gift that she cannot give herself? Horses cannot scratch their own backs. Do you think she would like it if we scratched her back?"

At this question, Nathan's eyes were soft and round. Instead of the "don't care" shrug, he nodded in agreement and reached up with me to the mare's spine. Together we scratched the length of her back with all our strength. The sad mare raised her head in utter delight. Her upper lip began to wiggle back and forth in pure equine gratitude.

"Nathan, look how much she likes that!" I laughed.

He saw the funny expression on her face and started laughing too.

"More, more, *more*," I encouraged. "We can't give her too much love!"

I reminded Nathan that only moments ago, she had moved away from us. Then, in gamelike fashion, I said, "Quick! Stop scratching and hide!" Before he knew what I meant, I spun around and jumped a few steps away and crouched down into the dirt.

He followed my actions. While huddled together, his expression told me that he thought I was a little crazy, but his grin confirmed that he was starting to have fun. He was beginning to trust me.

Shoulder to shoulder, a simple woman and a broken little boy knelt on the arena floor—waiting. The silence was broken with a soft sound, and then another. Footsteps. The sad mare was moving toward us. Together, we repeated the "scratch and hide" process until Nathan was laughing and saying, "Again! Again!" Without knowing it, he was acting out, literally showing me, exactly what *he* wanted—a true gift of love, given again and again.

During our game, I clarified the scene for Nathan. I reminded him of how earlier the mare had been so sad that she did not want our company; she did not want to be touched. She wanted to be left alone. Then, his persistent gift of love broke through her sadness. Because he refused to give up even when she did not respond right away, now she was coming to find him. Her despair had been lifted by his selfless actions.

"Look, Nathan, love is more than something you feel. It's also something you *do*. Real love does not quit when it's not loved back. Real love presses in and loves really well no matter what the response. Does that make sense?"

For the first time, my young friend looked at my face. His beautiful blue eyes locked on mine—and he nodded.

The rest of our time together was an honest display of three individuals—a middle-aged woman, an old horse and a hurting boy—all speaking the universal language of love and applying it to each other well.

Nathan took the scratching game to even greater heights by sitting on the mare's bare back. With the instruction that horses are very large and there is a lot of them to love, he sat forward first and scratched her shoulders and as far up her neck as he could reach. Then, he turned around and sat backward and scratched her rump and as far as his arms could stretch down each hind leg. We were thrilled to see the old horse's expression change from "leave me alone" to "I'm the most blessed horse on earth!"

A broken boy did that. He did it in minutes with the only gift he had—love.

While Nathan was still atop the mare enjoying the scratching game, I asked for some tack to be brought out for him. After a thorough grooming of the horse, Nathan tacked up his new friend. In minutes, he was trotting figure eights and laughing hysterically while trying to show me his best superhero impression. The boy who, only an hour earlier, screamed in my face to be left alone was now freely giving me high fives and hugs around the neck.

In return, I broke all the rules of modern etiquette and touched him on his shoulders, knees and hands. I hugged his neck, and once his helmet was off, I even ruffled his dark blond hair into a silly style so he would look more like Superman in a stiff wind.

From beyond the paneled fence behind me, his therapist softly repeated, "I don't believe it, I don't *believe* it!"

Indeed, when we do not believe, we do not see either. Unbelief is the stealer of sight. It is the root of nearly all blindness to the victories of God (see 1 Peter 1:8–9; John 20:29–31; 2 Corinthians 5:7).

The boy who earlier growled at me was now reaching for me with both arms, not because *my* love is great but because *Jesus'* love is great. And the sparks blowing off the unquenchable flame of Jesus' love in one heart flew into the dry tinder of another heart, igniting the gift of genuine hope.

Our time together ended with kisses on an old mare's muzzle and an enduring hug for me. Nathan even drew a fine picture of the three of us on a dry erase board. What I loved most about his impromptu artwork was the fact that he drew *all* of us, including the stick figure of himself, with big smiles on our faces.

Within the heart of this boy, for a moment—a brief moment—there was peace. Genuine pain was confronted with the genuine love of Jesus. There was no battle. Instead, His Spirit marched in and took ownership.

The following day I was scheduled to come speak at Nathan's school. It was a special education center and the last stop for troubled kids whose next destination would either be a juvenile prison or the psychiatric ward. Although this was far from a Christian school, the superintendent was a strong believer and gave me permission to speak freely of the only hope that could save them—the name of Jesus. She gave this permission knowing she could get fired for doing so. She was willing to take that bullet, the hit of losing her job, so the devastated kids in her care could hear the truth.

It was made known to me that these kids were so uncontrollable that the staff never let them all out at the same time for fear of a riot. As I walked to the front of the mob to share, I was aware of the entire faculty lining the perimeter walls in case violence broke out. But as He would have it, the only uncontrollable thing breaking out was the Holy Spirit delivering the almighty gift of Jesus' love.

There was no disrespect, jeering talk or inappropriate behavior. Instead, His presence rose like an unstoppable wave. It crushed through walls of hopelessness and flooded longing hearts with the uncontainable tide of His love. Those who rushed forward did not do so to riot—they came forward to pray. Several asked Jesus to wash, fill and heal their hearts and become their Lord. I cheered with heaven's host when I saw three newly redeemed lambs willingly snap large pentagram necklaces off their necks and throw them into the trash.

Afterward, I scanned the crowd, looking for Nathan. When I saw him standing in the back, I grinned at him.

He smiled back, then made his way to me.

"Hey, little man!" I exclaimed, hugging him tight in front of all who gathered around.

Once released, he motioned for me to bend down close so he could whisper in my ear. With my ear poised next to his lips, he asked in a hushed voice, "Do you like brownies?"

I laughed. "Is this a trick question? I *love* brownies!"

Nathan glanced from side to side as he reached deep into his front jeans pocket. After a few moments of fumbling, he pulled out a squashed, completely grease-soaked white napkin.

Looking directly at my face, he whispered, "I saved this for you."

With care, I unwrapped the oil-drenched tissue. Smashed within was a mutilated brownie. I looked at Nathan.

His eyes glittered with anticipation. Then, he grinned. I could feel my eyes warm with rising tears. My little food-obsessive buddy had given me his greatest gift: his dessert from the night before. During this time in his young life, it was what he valued most. It was his very best gift.

"Oh, my goodness! Nathan, can I just hug you?"

At the mention of my request—in front of all his hardened friends—he nodded like the happiest little bobblehead on the planet.

I pulled him close and whispered back, "Thank you, Nathan. Thank you. You're such a good boy, such a good, good boy. I'm so glad you're my friend."

Offering God's Greatest Gift to the World around You

Genuine love given fuels genuine love in return.

Sometimes it takes months. Sometimes it takes minutes. Because of God's untamable love, a broken little boy chose to give me the very best gift he could muster. When examined under the world's sense of value, Nathan's gift to me would have been meaningless, even disgusting, something to throw away. From my perspective, however, it was priceless, beautiful, something to treasure. Why? Because I understood how much value *he* placed on this gift and how much it cost him.

Within those hallowed two days, a hurting little boy was turned toward the undeniable power of genuine love. In the process, a new friendship was forged and sealed with a true gift.

This encounter magnifies the truth that sad mares and angry boys exist around each of us every day. Within our proximity are many who are crying out to be seen, to be loved toward the hope of Jesus. There are those in your midst who yearn for Jesus' deeper gift: His love, hope and redemption.

Jesus offers the perfect gift in every opportunity. How? His love always steps through the "right" answer to the *real* answer. His love always reaches beyond the "right" need to the *real* need. His love is more than a good gift—it is the *greatest* gift (see 1 Corinthians 13).

When it comes to human pain, there is only one true answer: "Oh, what a miserable person I am! Who will free me from this life that is dominated by sin and death? Thank God! The answer is in Jesus Christ our Lord" (Romans 7:24–25). If you are seeking hope for your broken heart, there *is* an answer—His name is Jesus.

In Matthew 11:28, Jesus speaks of how He reaches out for anyone who is hurting, beckoning everyone to come to Him. He encourages each of us to leave our places of pain and sorrow and come into His arms of hope. Jesus' love for all humanity is so deep, so pure, so vast that He gave the greatest gift of all time—His life as a sacrifice for all our sin and pain (see John 3:16–17).

On this day, perhaps the heart that is broken is yours.

Know that Jesus is passionate about your freedom, so much so that He gave His life to heal your brokenness. "O Lord, you are so good, so ready to forgive, so full of unfailing love for all who ask for your help" (Psalm 86:5). His desire is to help you, to draw you into a new friendship, a deep relationship forged within His heart and sealed with the greatest gift of all—His priceless love. This was and is His very best gift.

Friend, once you give Him all your heart, all your heart can be filled with all His love. Out of that complete restoration comes complete filling. Out of the "completely full" pours forth the overflow. And the overflow of His love through your life transforms the world around you.

This is the bedrock, the unshakable foundation of what it means to give. This is the limitless nature of God's wild giving.

ENCOUNTER HIM THROUGH *Prayer*

Lord Jesus,

It's Your genuine love within me that fuels genuine love in return. Your love is not a good gift; it's the greatest gift—always. Within my proximity are masses who are crying out to be seen and loved and to know the depth of Your saving grace. Because I know this can take minutes or months, I purpose to never give up.

And, may I never give up on my heart either. Right now, I raise before You all that is still broken within me. I acknowledge that You're passionate about my complete freedom. It's Your desire to draw me into a deeper friendship, a profound relationship, one sealed with the greatest gift—Your love for me, Your child.

Jesus, today I choose to let go of my hurting places and give You every part of me. Please heal and restore all my heart so I can be filled with all Your love.

I know that with Your complete restoration comes complete filling. Out of the "completely full" pours the overflow. It's the overflow through my life that transforms me continually—and the world around me—with Your beautiful, powerful, unstoppable love.

Today, I ask You, Lord, to fashion me into a pure-hearted conduit for Your glory. I choose to become a channel through which Your greatest gift—Your boundless compassion—pours out, completely unhindered by anything in me. I want to give as generously as You do. May my life become a mirror of Your wild giving.

PART THREE

Encountering His Restoration

Wild Faith

Faith shows the reality of what we hope for; it is
the evidence of things we cannot see.

Hebrews 11:1

Trust that has been practiced—applied again and again—
matures into faith. It is true.

Not long ago, I heard an evangelist say that he prayed for
healing over a thousand different people before God healed
one. His trust in God's healing power was tested heavily.
Not physically seeing the outcome of his continual prayers
did not deter him from pressing in and allowing his trust to
become galvanized into faith.

Faith is not something we can have just because we want
it. Faith is forged in the white-hot fire of trusting in God
more than ourselves—time and time again. Indeed, it is the
confident assurance that what we hope for *is* going to happen (see Hebrews 11:1).

For some, faith feels like taking a great leap without knowing where you will land—and trusting that God Himself is going to catch you. In all my life, not once have I seen a loving father gently toss his child up in the air and that child freak out in a flailing, screaming, clawing melee. I have seen only squeals of pure delight and the pleading for more. Children become so enveloped in faith that Dad will catch them that all they experience is the pure joy of simply being in his presence.

I want faith like that.

No wonder Jesus calls us to become like children in our walk with Him (see Matthew 18). Kids have a natural way of pursuing trust that leads to faith.

Second Corinthians 5:7 (NKJV) tells us to "walk by faith, not by sight." How much clearer can God be in calling us to trust Him enough to walk toward Him, on—over—through the impossible? The truth is, *impossible* is not even a word in God's vocabulary; it is only a word in mine when I choose not to trust Him. When the impossible arises within me, faith diminishes. When faith arises, the impossible evaporates. These two concepts cannot coexist within the heart of any believer.

We can only genuinely believe in *one*.

The Leap of Faith

Recently, I had the incredible opportunity of traveling to Eastern Europe to share the Gospel of Jesus Christ. Our five-woman team was comprised of a logistics manager, a translator, a worship leader, a prayer warrior, and I was tasked with the honor of sharing the message of hope in Jesus.

We had traveled through much of Moldova, one of the poorest nations in Europe, and were making our way through

Romania. During our time there, we had the sweet privilege of speaking in a midsized church in the stunning medieval city of Sighișoara. A sea of red ceramic rooftops and brightly colored homes surrounded the church like a warm embrace. All lay far below the impressive silhouette of ancient citadel towers built in the twelfth century atop the highest knoll. The entire old city was constructed on a breathtaking slope that ran down to the Tarnâva Mare River. The region itself seemed to revel in its beautiful history of worshiping God.

After an anointed time of singing together and an enthusiastic, Spirit-filled message, I offered the call to come forward for prayer. Nearly the entire assembly flooded into the center aisle in a slightly frenzied crush. To handle the crowd, we formed three prayer teams across the front of the sanctuary and began the poignant process of receiving each woman individually.

My translator was a descendant of the Gypsy race and culture. She had stunning green eyes framed by a tumbling mass of long, curly black hair. Yet as beautiful as she was on the outside, her passionate heart for sharing Jesus with her people was far more so. During our hasty introduction, every ounce of her short stature surrounded me with a giant hug as she declared, "Sister, you look Gypsy! You have dark hair and green eyes too!"

Side by side, we worked like field doctors diagnosing the source of pain and releasing the authority of the Spirit of the living God to heal it.

One tiny elderly woman hobbled up in open sandals. Her small, wide feet were so crippled with severe bunions that she could hardly walk. We prayed fervently over her heart and her wayward family. Through tears she shared her gratitude. But the Spirit was not finished. He wanted to heal her feet too. We shared with her that Jesus loves her so much that He wanted to restore not only her heart and family but her twisted feet as well. Following the Spirit where *He* wanted to go, we asked if we could remove her sandals and anoint her feet with oil. She nodded enthusiastically.

I saw a picture in my mind of my hand under her foot, cradling it, with each of my fingertips aligned with each of her toes. While we prayed in this position, she started to speak in an elevated and excited tone. Without warning, she jumped up and hurried down the aisle back to her friends. As her friends encircled her, I watched as she lifted each of her bare feet and pointed at them, showing them to those who had come with her.

I shot a questioning glace at my translator.

She smiled back. "She's telling them, 'The pain is gone! The pain is gone!'"

Resembling nearly all those before her, the next woman in line came forward with a heavy countenance. She was greatly concerned for her alcoholic son and his four young children. Because he spent all his earnings on drinking, her beloved grandchildren were starving. They depended on her to bring them any food she could gather. This was her daily gift to her family—until the pain in her lower back and legs became so great that she could no longer walk. Now in her sixties, the diminished woman explained that her pain was so great that she could no longer attend church either. She was grateful that her friends, sensing this was a special night, came to her home and all but carried her into the church. Romanian women are so humble. On this night, she did not come forward for herself—she came because she wanted prayer for her son to know Jesus. She also requested protection and provision for her grandchildren that they would not starve in the process.

After a tearful rally of prayer, our heavyhearted friend felt encouraged enough to hug us in gratitude. Again, the Holy Spirit spoke that we were not finished. Once more, He wanted us to follow Him—where *He* wanted to go—to restore her body as well. We shared what He was speaking and asked if we could anoint her bare lower back with oil. She agreed readily and gave us greater access by bending over in her chair so that her chin was nearly on her knees. With our oiled hands on her back, I spoke out all that He was speaking over her. While her face was still down, she relayed that she could feel heat coming into her back.

Suddenly, she shot up completely straight. She glanced quickly between my face and our translator, then started to speak in a rapid and astonished tone. The translator clarified, "She says, 'I'm burning! My legs are on fire! I'm burning up! Fire is burning down my legs!'"

Together, we told her this was the power of the Holy Spirit coming upon her. We shared that He had heard her continual prayer over her broken family and was healing them. But He also wanted to heal her. The heat in her body was His presence coming in and restoring her legs. His love was renewing and reestablishing what was broken, not only in her heart but in her physical body as well.

I watched our friend's face fill with an expression that reflected wonder, fear and amazement. Her deep-brown eyes were wide and pinballing, as if documenting each new sensation she was feeling. Her mouth was slightly parted open with the smallest smile of pure awe. Her hands rose and fell over her thighs as if she were touching a hot stove repeatedly.

Our prayer over her finished with the humble phrase, "By the authority of the name of Jesus, receive this healing from the heavenly Father, the One who loves you most." Together, we helped our new friend stand up.

Subconsciously, she shifted her weight back and forth between her feet. I took delight in watching her beautiful eyes get bigger and bigger. We hugged, laughed and kissed each other's cheeks. To document the moment, we even took a picture of us standing arm in arm.

Again, I felt the prompting of the Holy Spirit.

He moved me to ask something specific of her—something that would strengthen her faith in a covenant way. I explained that in the Bible when Jesus and the apostles prayed over people, they often asked those who were healed to do something that was impossible for them to do before. Jesus asked one to pick up his mat and start walking; He told another to show himself to the priest. One man, while he was still blind, was asked to find his way to a pool and wash his eyes—then he could see.

I looked into my friend's incredulous face and asked her point-blank, "Is there something that you could not do before that you're feeling Jesus would have you do now?"

Deep thought sent her gaze meandering up toward the ceiling. I realized that all this communication was happening through a translator. She might be struggling to understand what was being asked of her.

Soon, she looked back at my face and smiled brightly. Apparently, she had come to a conclusion. I watched as she raised both of her arms in the air and shouted, "Hallelujah!" Her chosen response was not quite what I meant, but it was sweet and powerful nonetheless.

Once again, we hugged and kissed each other's cheeks multiple times in the endearing Romanian way. Finally, it was the moment to say good-bye and move on to the next woman in line.

She took a few halting steps toward the door. Then, she stopped. I was aware that she had passed behind me and walked up the stairs that led to the stage. As I started to engage the next woman, my newly healed friend moved so that she was in my line of sight right behind the woman I was speaking to.

I watched over the current woman's shoulder as my new friend crouched down to level her eyes with mine. I turned my head slightly to engage her fully. She was staring right at my eyes, as if she wanted me to "see" her. With our gazes locked, I turned my head toward her and smiled, indicating that she had my full attention.

She was crouching on the stage, which was three feet higher than the main room floor. I watched this elderly woman stand up to her full height, stare straight down at me and then jump. She jumped off the stage—literally!

After landing spryly on the room floor, she popped up like a Jack-in-the-box. Again, she looked right at me. But this time, she flashed a dazzling smile and then winked at me.

She got it totally. She completely understood everything I had asked her earlier and then carried it out in a miraculous "book of Acts" fashion. I watched her stride down the church center aisle like a twenty-year-old. Without hesitation, she hit the double doors with both hands and pushed them out of her way. Everything about her new demeanor shouted, *Look out, world! I'm back!*

It was a leap of faith—a literal leap of faith.

A broken elderly woman was carried into church by her friends. Within this place, she had an encounter with our wild God. Her heart was restored, her body was restored, her faith was restored. Moments later, the same woman strode out whole, like a young gun on a mission.

How long she had been in pain is unknown. How many times she had asked the Lord for healing is unknown. What *is* known is that she had the faith to ask God, again, for help. She did not reduce her life to self-imposed defeat. She did not stay trapped in the realm of, *God has not answered my prayers all this time, so why would He start now?* Instead, in that beautiful moment, she mirrored Jesus' parable about the woman who would not take no for an answer: "One day Jesus told his disciples a story to show that they should *always pray and never give up*" (Luke 18:1, emphasis added).

This woman *never* gave up.

For as long as she had been in pain, there remained enough faith in God to believe that He could still answer her plea for help—right up until the moment that He did.

The Leap from Our Impossible into His Arms of Possible

When it comes to faith in Christ, the only way to fail is to quit.

Please understand that I am *not* saying we can earn our salvation or God's favor. I *am* saying that when it comes to matters of faith, we often give up way too easily. As in most things God is calling us to trust Him with, faith's greatest enemy is found in our eyes—it is called shortsightedness. We pray a few times, maybe for a few weeks, a few months or even a few years, and when God does not answer our prayers, we give up. Somehow, we take verses that tell us plainly to pray at all times, pray without ceasing, pray on every occasion in the power of the Holy Spirit, and we relegate them into mere suggestions (see Philippians 4:6; 1 Thessalonians 5:17; Ephesians 6:18). When we do this, we demote the fire of our faith to something that rises before God as lukewarm.

But the wild faith of our God is anything but lukewarm. It is a raging inferno that nothing in this universe can stop.

Genuine, living, growing faith moves beyond believing into knowing God will act. It is not hesitant—it knows. Moses *knew* God would act when he raised his staff over the Red Sea (see Exodus 14:21). Joshua *knew* God would act when he circled Jericho seven times and shouted (see Joshua 6). Elijah *knew* God would act when he challenged all the prophets of Baal (see 1 Kings 18). Jesus *knew* God would act when He submitted His life to the cross (see Luke 22–23; John 19). A broken woman in a poor country knew God would act when she stood to her feet and then jumped off a stage.

They proved their faith by their actions. Each leapt into the presence of God, *before the miracle*, and trusted Him for the outcome. These men and women did not measure out their faith by the portion or quantity they had already seen, because that is not really faith. Seeing is not believing—believing first is seeing (see 2 Corinthians 3:16).

If God calls us to take that leap of faith, we can know it will be God who will catch us.

Like the loving father who tosses his child gently up in the air, if God tosses us up, He will catch us. If we are willing to take that leap of faith into our impossible, that is when we experience His miraculous breakthrough into all that is possible *through Him*.

In Luke 8:22–25, we read of Jesus being roused awake by His panicking disciples. He then rebukes the wind and the waves. By the authority of His command, the storm stopped and all was calm. Then He turned to face His disciples and asked them, "Where is your faith?" (v. 25).

Great question. Indeed, where is *my* faith?

Like the disciples, when challenges and storms come, we can consign our faith in only one of two places: in ourselves or in our Savior. We can put our faith in our own understanding, our own experience, our own emotion and our own strength to get the job done. Unfortunately, this choice emerges from human logic, not faith, and it always reveals foundational unbelief. When we choose to face our storms balanced primarily on our knowledge, eventually we will collapse into despair. Or we can place our faith in our Savior. This decision emerges from the bedrock of trust and leads to responding out of truth. This always reveals foundational faith. When we set our hearts firmly on faith in Him, we will be at rest no matter what we face.

Unlike the disciples, Jesus was not upset by the storm—He was asleep *in* the storm. Our Lord was so at peace in His Father's love because of His faith that He could sleep in the face of destruction.

Like Jesus, we should all pursue trusting our amazing heavenly Father so much that we, too, can rest in His presence through any storm. This is where wild faith begins.

ENCOUNTER HIM THROUGH *Prayer*

Lord Jesus,

One of the greatest questions You asked mankind was, Where is your faith? *In this moment, I'm compelled to wonder,* Where is my faith?

Have my eyes become so dimmed by the lull of short-sightedness that I've quit Your hallowed pursuit of praying and believing for breakthrough? Has the fire of my faith become so demoted that it smolders before Your throne as little more than lukewarm?

Enough of my complacency! When it comes to faith, the only way to fail is to quit. Jesus, I refuse to quit! No more "back door" prayers. Instead, I confess my pride, my fear and my apathy to You. May they burn up in the inferno that is Your very presence. I welcome Your wild faith within me. It isn't lukewarm; it's a raging blaze that nothing in this universe can stop. It isn't hesitant. It doesn't waver before the impossibilities of men. It tramples over merely believing into knowing You will act.

King Jesus, today, I let go of my "faithless boat" and jump toward You. I choose to leap through my impossible into the miraculous breakthrough of all that is possible through You. I acknowledge that when You call me to leap, it will be You who catches me.

Lord, right now I yield all of me into Your omniscient hands. You're a loving Father. I trust You to toss me as high as You choose. Where's my faith? It's in You. I have faith that You will catch me. Because I choose to believe this truth, when the storms come, I, too, will rest in the arms of my Father.

9

Wild Gentleness

Bartimaeus threw aside his coat, jumped up, and
came to Jesus. "What do you want me to do for
you?" Jesus asked. "My Rabbi," the blind man
said, "I want to see!" And Jesus said to him, "Go,
for your faith has healed you." Instantly the man
could see, and he followed Jesus down the road.

Mark 10:50–52

The wild gentleness of our God is easy to find.

The moment we dare to turn off the well-worn path of our
human understanding and control—and follow *His* Spirit—is
the same moment we experience the vast depth of who the
Author of gentleness is.

God is gentle, and gentle is our God.

We cannot know gentleness apart from the One who created it—or the One apart from His gentleness. It is an element

of His very nature. It is a component of His heart. The more we pursue His presence, the more we discover the limitless expanse of His gentleness.

Found within these daring strides of pursuit is the almighty power to heal on a foundational level. By choosing to follow the Spirit of gentleness where He *wants* to lead, prison walls shatter beneath the weight of His infinite freedom.

Choosing Nearness to God over Suffering as a Path to Freedom

My first impressions of John were formed in a single firm handshake.

He was not tall, but he was huge. I am not a small woman and I do not have small hands, but his callused hand surrounded and crushed mine like a bear paw. His shoulders were wide and his chest was deep. He bore the "no neck" look of a man who, for decades, had used his own body as his primary working tool.

John was a rancher by trade. Tanned skin covered the thick muscle this hardworking man had earned. He was a dude, a man's man, a guy you could count on to get the job done.

Even though we were nearly the same height, I am pretty sure this guy could have crushed me with a sneeze. Yet as notable as his appearance was, what moved me most about him were his eyes. Standing out in complete defiance of his imposing persona were playful eyes. I was delightfully surprised the first time I saw John smile. When his thick bronzed cheeks mashed up around his eyes, they shone bright with the impishness of a child.

I liked John immediately.

We had been introduced at a local church where I had spoken. He had come forward after the service for prayer over what he believed Jesus was calling him to do—build a working ranch for troubled youth. Our combined passion for broken kids drew us to our knees. The prayer that flowed from this powerful, compassionate man was pure, strong and heartfelt. In the most straightforward way, he wanted shattered youth to understand that no matter what their past held, they could still belong to a father—the Father who loves them most.

The same evening we met, I agreed to join John the following day for a special assignment. He hoped that Judy, my dear friend and faithful assistant, and I would join him in praying over a piece of property that he felt the Lord was drawing him toward. John was painfully aware that in this tropic region all property was astronomically expensive, light-years beyond the reach of his meager rancher's wage.

But truth is truth—God owns all, and He dispenses what is already His when He chooses. Our job is not to figure out how He will do the miraculous, but to trust and believe that He can.

Judy and I met John at an easy-to-find central location. Then we slid into his car, and he drove the remainder of the way.

When we came to a stop, we all stepped out into a realm that could have been heaven itself. The entire property was swathed in lush natural grass and sedges. The grass was so deep that it bent and waved before the wind in extravagant patterns.

We climbed to the top of a windswept knoll. From this high place, all creation plunged downward into deep grassy folds toward the ocean. The view was so expansive that it stretched the boundary of human comprehension. Hallowed was the ground upon which we stood. Earth, sky and sea united together to give glorious witness to the One who made it all. From this place, the vast expanse of dancing grass was mesmerizing, all waving in lavish worship before God.

For this heart, places like these help to clarify and inspire the definition of true worship. They serve as an inspiration and reflection of the glorious, wild God we serve.

Jolted back to the task at hand, John produced a large map of what could become a future ranch. We felt led by the Spirit to place the map on the top of the hill and then walk around it in prayer. The wind was so powerful on the ocean side of the incline that had we not secured the map with stones, it might have taken flight to parts unknown.

Finally, it was time to join creation in worship and prayer. Together, we made vague circles around the map, each praying through whatever the Spirit laid on our hearts. Over time, the wind became so violent that we took refuge on the leeward side of the slope. Continuing our mission, we knelt down in the deep grass. Sheltered from the howling wind overhead, we could now hear each other pray.

Our requests were completely focused on the possibility of a new ranch, along with wisdom, clarity, peace, redemption and complete trust in following the Holy Spirit. At random, John, Judy and I would speak out and pray through whatever He desired. Although lulls are not uncommon in group prayer, this lull . . . *was*.

There was a distinct stirring. What I sensed was not the wind. It was not the grass waving around us. It was Him.

He wanted all three of us to go deeper.

Holy Spirit, lead me was my silent prayer. What followed was even more powerful, even more beautiful than the vast glory that surrounded us.

God does not want to heal and fill only part of our heart. He wants to heal and fill all of our heart. Yet He cannot fill a place within us that is already filled with . . . *us*. Our sin, our fear, our guilt, our pain, our bitterness, our unforgiveness, our complacency and our pride must be poured out willingly before Him. We must choose to let go of our baggage so our hands will be free to receive His blessing, His abundance, His freedom.

At this point, John was kneeling between Judy and me. He responded to our gentle encouragements and began to pour out his heart. Slowly, he dared to leave the well-worn path that others can see, venturing deeper into a place within that was growing darker with each step. His body responded to the encroaching dungeon by getting smaller and smaller. I watched as this hulk of a man compressed himself into an incomprehensibly small form.

We were getting closer to the ignition of his pain. I looked over his broad back at Judy. She felt it too. Led by the Spirit, she mouthed, *His childhood.*

Reaching over, I placed the palm of my hand on the center of his back. This single act of compassion became the Spirit's weapon of war to attack an enemy stronghold. Despite the wind, sweat soaked through his shirt and formed under my hand. Through my palm, I could feel John begin to tremble as his back tightened into something that was no longer flesh. Deep was crying out to deep. The Spirit of the living God was calling to the Spirit living within His son, a son He beckoned to drop the baggage and come home.

Nudged by the Spirit, I leaned in and whispered, "Speak it out."

Habitually, the enemy uses the shame of personal revelation to keep our prison doors firmly locked. Our own humiliation, embarrassment and fear become the self-appointed prison guards of our own generational sin and trauma. But those guards, those doors, those black walls are no match against the raw power of the wild gentleness of our God.

John's trembling escalated into waves of full-blown body tremors. Somehow, he balanced on his wide knees in a fetal position, crushing his clenched fists between his forehead and the earth. As if trying to climb into and hide within a smaller version of himself, my friend began to writhe. The power of our gentle God was breaking through. John's bear-paw hands had tightened into white-knuckled fists. He pressed them with such force against his forehead that a lesser skull might have shattered. He was forcing his body into such a tiny form that I expected to hear bones break.

Then I heard it.

Through jaws drawn into a teeth-shattering clench, a tortured growl escaped. The prison walls had been breached. What followed was something I would not have believed was humanly possible had I not been present. From deep within this massive man rose the tortured cry of a terrified little boy. High-pitched wails rose in wave after wave until they crossed the threshold of piercing screams—the screams of a boy, a baby boy.

Carried forward by each shuddering, painful surge, the screams escalated into the realm of such relived terror that his child's voice began to shred and crack apart, unable to go any higher. Every scream brought what felt like electrocution to my soul. Scorching hot adrenaline burned through my momma's heart. These were the horrifying screams of a child who believed he was going to die.

When his voice could go no higher, when the tears could not fall any faster, when the crushing stress of concealing a secret could be held no longer, the prison walls fell.

"Daaaaaddy . . . Daaaaaddy. Why? Why are you beating me? Why? Why are you hurting me? I love you, Daddy! I love you!"

There it was—the shackles.

As the awful truth of a baby boy's chains were revealed, so was the Chain Breaker.

Deep within the realm of a little boy's torture, heavy black chains of restraint covered their iron eyes, unable to look upon the new laser beam of glorious light that poured over them. Once revealed, they started to dissolve. Slowly, every hideous link turned to liquid when caught within the wondrous inferno of love burning from the Father's eyes as He looked upon His son—and the *son looked back*.

From the enemy there was no fight. There was no struggle. There was no war. Waged in the realm we cannot see, the ensuing battle amounted to little more than a dark, toxic vapor evaporating before the morning Son.

As he knelt, drenched in sweat and soaked with tears, John's screams were unleashed and replaced with the deep, drawing breaths of freedom. Crumpling with release, this little boy wanted to rock, so with our arms reaching across his back, Judy and I rocked him, a baby boy who finally understood he was a beloved son of God.

Just like that, it was over. A generational prison collapsed in a moment and was spirited away by the enduring trade winds of release.

Atop that windswept hill, all that remained was a herculean little boy blinking up into the streaming light of a new day, a new life, a new heart. Although it was always available, this was the day John embraced new freedom in the Daddy who loves him most. Now all that swirled around us was the unconditional love of the Father streaming through the very presence of the Holy Spirit.

John's forgiveness of his father was immediate. He had fought his entire life to conceal and control his pain. Yet in one honest moment, he chose nearness to God over his suffering. In that powerful instant, the Holy Spirit within him arced to God the Father and back again, and fear was exchanged for freedom.

The previous terror of a boy was replaced with spontaneous thanksgiving from a man. The enormous hands that were once filled with painful baggage were now raised high in worship. Screams were replaced with shouts of praise to the One who gives freedom to anyone who asks.

Forever imprinted on my mind is the powerful image of John rising to his feet atop a gusty summit, lifting open palms toward the heavens and shouting, "Jeeeeesus, Jeeeeesus, thank You!" On that day, under a blue sky, it began to rain. Falling all around us rained great drops of freedom.

Jumping into the River of the Holy Spirit and Following Him

As mentioned earlier in this book, Pastor Surprise once said, "The Holy Spirit is like a great and mighty river. You do not tell the river where to go. No, you do not do this. Instead, you jump into the river . . . and you go where He takes you."

We thought we were going up the hill to pray over property.

Right up until the Holy Spirit redirected, we were completely focused on the plan. Although it was a good plan, it was not His complete plan. It would have been easy to march through toward part of His goal and miss the breakthrough He had intended all along. From the Spirit's perspective, this day was never about prayer over the plans of men—the plan was always about moving the man into prayer.

A continual yielding to the Spirit's continual movement is all He desires from those who are His. This is the powerful journey toward the wild gentleness of our God.

In the quiet of that evening the Holy Spirit clarified, *Listen to Me. Follow Me. Trust Me. You thought you were going to pray over property—when all along I wanted you to pray over a prisoner. Those who are willing to follow Me will become the simple, mighty vessels of the living God. In this willing place, all will see My glory.*

Jesus did not endure the cross so we could stay in prison.

Jesus came to this world with one thing in mind—to set prisoners free. Willingly, He left heaven's glory, became a man and walked among us. He not only became acquainted with our sorrows, but He took them all—all shame, all suffering, all pain, all sin. He bore this crushing blackness to the cross . . . and died there. But He did not stay in the grave. When Jesus rose from the dead, He broke the lock on the prison door of suffering and sin, and that hideous door can never be closed again.

Each one of us will spend time in the prison of suffering. And when we do, there is no better time to realize that the door is open. All we need to do is reach for the hand of the One who has always been reaching for us and step out into the freedom that He has purchased for all.

Jesus calls us to exchange the shackles of our grief for the freedom of His grace.

He did for a blind man named Bartimaeus. In Mark 10, Jesus was traveling to Jericho. Bartimaeus shouted over the crowd for Jesus' help. Those around him tried to shame him into silence. But Jesus heard his cries for help and stopped everything. He asked Bartimaeus to come to Him, then healed him in front of all present.

Perhaps the only difference in this story today is that the voices shaming us into silence before Jesus come from our own lips. Yet, like Bartimaeus, if we forsake our comfort, our pride, our potential embarrassment and follow the leading of the Holy Spirit to pursue Jesus, He will stop everything. He will ask us to come to Him, and then He heals us in front of all present.

Because of what Jesus has already done, the shackles of our past do not hold us—we hold them. We can come to Jesus every minute of every day, and He will stop everything and heal us.

Our debt of pain has been paid.

"For God says, 'At just the right time, I heard you. On the day of salvation, I helped you.' Indeed, the 'right time' is now. Today is the day of salvation" (2 Corinthians 6:2).

Today is the day of salvation. In this moment, your grief can be redeemed for His grace.

Just like John, you can exchange your black debt for His loving freedom—right now—because of the wild gentleness of our God.

ENCOUNTER HIM THROUGH *Prayer*

Lord Jesus,

Over two thousand years ago, You destroyed the power of sin, death and the grave on the cross. Because of this fact, I recognize that the only one keeping me in a prison of pain . . . is me. The black shackles of my past do not hold me—I hold them.

Light and darkness cannot occupy the same place within my heart. Jesus, I cannot hold onto my pain and reach for You at the same time. I can't actively cling to my brokenness while crying out for You to rescue me.

You have rescued me already.

Your empty tomb destroyed the power of the enemy to control me and inflict pain on me. Whatever past woundings I'm currently experiencing are those I'm giving my adversary permission to wield against me.

Jesus, when You rose from the grave, You rolled the stone away from Your tomb . . . and mine as well. Because of this truth, I see that my black dungeon has only three sides. Nothing is keeping me in this place of pain but me. All I need to do is reach out for Your hand of hope—the loving hand You've extended to me every minute of my life.

With my hand in Yours, I will speak out every dark, shameful, angry, bitter, fearful, prideful place. And in so doing, I will see the heavy black chains of my imprisonment evaporate in revelation as I turn my eyes from focusing on them to focusing only on You.

Precious Savior, in this moment I choose to reach out and embrace Your wild gentleness. From this day forward, I covenant with You to not allow my past to determine my future. You, Jesus, are my future.

10

Wild Love

Anyone who does not love does not know God,
for God is love.

1 John 4:8

Love is the greatest gift of all.

The genuine love of God is the greatest gift to mankind in all of human history. Why? Because He Himself is love, He is the Author and Creator, the Provider and the Supplier. God the Father proved how vitally important His love is by redeeming this fallen world with the embodied love of His Son. He chose love over all other attributes.

This is what Jesus desires most for every heart—to pursue His love, to be filled with His love, to pour out His love. Most of my life I have had the order wrong. I always had the *doing for* God in front of the *being with* God, not understanding that everything I seek to accomplish for His glory comes naturally when I remain in His love (see John 15:10).

Being *in* Christ will always supply the doing *for* Christ.

When it comes to the wild love of our God, the doing always comes out of the knowing, not the other way around. Jesus Himself states this truth in Matthew 6:33: "Seek the Kingdom of God *above all else*, and live righteously, and he will give you everything you need" (emphasis added).

God does not want our leftovers. He wants to be first. When we choose to move all other things aside and place Him in the center of our hearts—and remain in this place—our life becomes His kingdom. Our heart becomes the King's domain. And within His domain, He has rule and authority to express His love through us in whatever way He chooses.

The more we understand the wild love of our God, the more we will understand why Jesus came to this earth: "to seek and save those who are lost" (Luke 19:10). His incomprehensible love drove Him to choose the cross. His uncontainable love broke the power of death and the grave. His untamable love descended upon the apostles in the Upper Room. And His extreme, indefinable love still fills the hearts of those who commit to pursue Him above all else.

This love is so vast that no reach of human understanding can contain it. It does not fit in any man-made box of logic. Instead, it flows like a mighty, unstoppable flood wherever He desires. And it heals every life it contacts.

Pursuing the "More" of Jesus' Love

The moment I saw Aly, my heart dropped. The vibrant, strong, charismatic rancher I once knew was gone.

The woman approaching me was so physically broken that the straightforward act of walking was no longer possible. What remained of her ambulatory ability was only possible with the substantial support of her husband's arm on one side, and a service dog's strong back on the other.

Amid Aly's struggle to walk into the main yard of the ranch, she looked up to see me watching her. Her immediate response was genuine. True to her indomitable nature, she flashed a bright smile. Despite her effort to choose joy, something dark was lurking behind her warm countenance. Although her face brightened into a familiar expression, the raw pain behind her eyes was unmistakable, like a lost electric current arcing between us. Beyond the depth of words, her anguish seared into my soul.

Compassion filled my heart, and apparently my countenance as well. One look at my face was all it took for the anchorage of her stoic bravery to be ripped from its moorings. In a hail of quiet words, her tale of woe added to the growing scorch mark within my spirit.

Aly explained that earlier she had fallen backward and broken her wrist. The pain of that injury was so intense that she didn't realize until later that she had also severely injured her lower back. She sought medical help multiple times, only to be misdiagnosed an equal number of times. Left to languish in agony, her only recourse for the pain in her lower back and left leg were powerful pain-suppressing drugs.

Finally, the pain was so excruciating that she was, again, rushed to receive medical care. While Aly lay flat on her stomach, the attending physician noticed something that all the others had missed—a large bulge protruding through the muscle of her lower left back.

The phantom protrusion was the outcome of an injury that produced lumbosacral plexopathy. This rare condition affected interwoven nerve bundles that deadened areas of her leg. The result was extreme pulsating pain through her lower back and down her leg. Over time, the nerves had been damaged to such a degree that her left leg was withering from lack of innervation, circulation and use.

Held in the vise grip of paralyzing pain, Aly had been confined to a bed or wheelchair for six months. Surgery relieved some of her pain, which enabled her to start physical therapy and learn to use crutches. Even still, her left leg was no longer usable. The ensuing atrophy was catastrophic. Her leg had lost two inches of its former length and over four inches of total circumference. Her condition was so dire that a portion of the medical community intimated the possible need for an amputation.

Surgery, intense physical therapy and a service dog had gotten her back on her feet—or foot. At this point, she had been sent home. All forward momentum had ceased, and medically there was little else that could be done. She was left to carry on, as is, in searing pain from a dying leg.

Within our conversation, she had shed no tears over her agonizing plight . . . until she mentioned the children. Aly and her husband, James, were the founders of a similar ministry called Grace Falls Farm. Together, they had been serving the Lord faithfully with rescued horses to reach the fractured hearts of hurting children, including their own two adopted girls.

Now, her only participation in the ministry she was called by her Father to lead was to lie in bed or sit in a wheelchair and listen. Daily, she could hear from outdoors the children ask repeatedly if she was all right and when they could see "Mrs. Aly" again. One little lamb even pleaded, "If I could just see her and give her a hug, everything will be okay."

But everything was not okay.

Aly's body was badly broken. Medical practitioners had sent her home to languish within a black prison of immeasurable pain. Aly was no longer able to engage in the ministry she loved. Instead, she was left behind, a mere spectator of her own life, a lonely shadow of the woman she once was. Her mental anguish was equally severe. More than once, she confided to James that she struggled with the desire to live.

Now Aly stood before me, balanced completely on her right leg. She was breathless from the exertion needed to move from her nearby car to where I stood, something the rest of us did without thought. For her, this herculean feat was accomplished with the help of her husband's support on her left side and a beautiful German shepherd on her right.

Recently, she had rescued her dog, Rook, from certain destruction. He had been picked up as a stray. After failing a temperament pinch test, he was slated to be destroyed the following day. Aly's immediate interventions saved his life. Now, with six months of training, Rook was returning the debt of love by wearing a full-body vest with a large heavy bar arching up in a semicircle over his shoulders. The bar was nearly the height of Aly's hip. With a tight grip on the bar, she would lurch most of her body weight onto his back, then swing her healthy leg forward while her left leg drug behind. For my once-strong-and-energetic friend, this carefully orchestrated motion now constituted one single step.

Following the compassionate urging of Rachel, our similar ministries coordinator, Aly and James agreed to sojourn to our ranch for our annual leadership conference, called DEEPER—Jesus first. From across this great country and beyond, guests were streaming in all around us.

There, in the midst of the excited swirl, I embraced my shattered friend.

After holding her for a while, I whispered in her ear, "I would love to pray with you sometime this week. Can we make that happen?"

Slowly releasing our embrace, she looked directly into my eyes with absolute intention and nodded. "Yes, I would *love* that."

The conference was filled to the brim with the beauty, power and wonder of our God. Hearts were strengthened, friendships were reinforced and lives were recentered before the Lord of all. It was the final night of the conference and the last evening the entire group would be together.

After dinner, most of the attendees were getting ready to engage in worship inside the main barn as the sun headed toward the jagged Central Oregon horizon. Some gathered outside around several fire pits, and many others sat in groups, each trying to squeeze out the last few droplets of merely being together.

With all the classes for the day completed, my main mission on this night was to locate Aly and James and fulfill my promise to pray with them. While searching through the crowd, it was not lost on my heart that many of the staff and I had been led to fast and pray fervently over this conference. We all had a powerful sense from the Holy Spirit that He desired breakthrough—a breakthrough of His love into the strongholds within the lives of those attending this event.

When I found James and Aly, I asked that we might move to the office porch for a bit more privacy. Once we settled in, we were instantly beset by others who were unaware of our need for a quieter place. We ended up moving to several different locations on the ranch, but each ended with the same sweet results. Finally, in an attempt to find a quiet space, I led my friends to the very back of the ranch. I was hopeful that we could pray together up on the lookout deck. Its elevation offered privacy and a spectacular view of the setting sun.

While slowly making our way up to the lookout, I was aware that my beloved friend Judy had "shadowed" us. She understood where we were going to pray, and she moved farther up the hill above us. Like a silent sentry, she took her position on the highest place on the ranch—under the cross. From this hallowed place, she prayed over us.

Dulled by fatigue and the quest to find a spot to pray, I did not fully comprehend how hard it would be for my broken friend to negotiate the twenty steps that led up to our destination. Once I had realized my mistake, Aly rebuked my suggestion to find another place and pressed into the challenge.

I watched in awe as she chose joy and tenacity over her obvious pain. Each step was a mighty test of sheer will. The nature of her injury had stolen her ability to use her left leg. The strength and balance of the leg was destroyed, and she no longer had sensation of any kind in her left foot.

Unable to put weight on her withered leg, Aly leaned heavily on the steel bar fastened to the harness connected to Rook's back. She would then hop up the step with her right leg and ask her faithful dog to help drag her left leg behind them.

Knowing I had caused this laborious process made it nauseating to watch.

Aly repeated the "hop and drag" progression until she stood flushed and breathless on the lookout deck. Glancing at me, she flashed an indomitable grin and puffed, "You know . . . that I'm not gonna . . . make it down. I'll have to sit . . . on my backside . . . and scoot!"

Finally, together in a quiet, peaceful place, we talked until the sun slipped below the horizon. With the western sky filling with color and worship music pouring out from the barn below, it was time to pray.

True to her unconquerable spirit, Aly said, "Wait! Let me get ready!" With an awkward and certainly painful effort, she lowered herself down from her chair until she was kneeling on the old board deck. "Okay, *now* I'm ready!"

Following the lead of the Holy Spirit, I knelt between James and Aly and placed my hands on the back of their necks. With heads bowed, they each prayed beautiful, powerful, selfless petitions. I finished by asking the Father for a deeper anointing of His Spirit over their relationship with Him, their hearts, their marriage, their health and their ministry. The power of His love filling that moment rained down in the form of abundant tears from all of us.

Slowly, we helped each other up to our feet. Like a Spirit-filled exclamation point, we fell into a tearful group embrace. Our bodies followed what our hearts had already done in spirit.

After releasing them both, I started to move toward the top of the stairs so I could assist Aly down. Before I could even cover the six-foot distance, I felt something like electricity bolt through my being. Simultaneously, I heard the Holy Spirit say, *Stop! I'm going to heal her.*

I turned to face Aly and told her what I had experienced. Her equally electrified response was an exuberant, "Yes, *yes!* He *is* going to heal me!"

Something I have noticed about learning how to follow the Spirit is that rarely will He do the same thing twice—perhaps because He knows that we would create a how-to formula and follow the recipe instead of Him. For this reason, I have learned to ask Him what *He* wants to do.

In this situation, I felt impressed to anoint our hands with oil—Aly's too. We were to layer our hands over the surgical scar on her lower back. Aly felt led to lie flat on the old wooden deck with her face down. In this position, she also placed one of her hands with ours, palm up.

The prayer that followed began like many others in a plea for healing. But something started to change. The air around us felt beautifully heavy, weighted, literally saturated with the palpable presence of the Holy Spirit.

Within my soul, I could hear the words, *Command! Take command! Command My power!*

I cannot describe the words of the prayer that flowed out next—only what I saw. I am still unsure whether my eyes were open or closed. A narrow shaft of light blazed down, cleaving the twilight. It went through our hands and into her back, covering her left buttock. Then it streaked down the back of Aly's leg to her knee.

I could hear myself say, "I can see light!"

From her facedown position, Aly responded, "I can feel it! It's like liquid sunshine pouring down! I can feel burning! My leg is burning!"

Around and around our prayers swirled, rising up like an unseen vortex, an invisible herald of adoration for the one true God. Our prayer finished with the simple statement, "Receive this healing from Jesus." With that, James and I pulled Aly up to her feet in one single motion.

I watched in wonder as my friend allowed her weight—for the first time in more than a year—to move over to her left leg. Then she exclaimed suddenly, "Hey, hey! I can feel my foot! I can feel my foot!" Her wide eyes scrunched shut in what looked like concentration. "Wait, wait! I . . . I can wiggle my toes!" Again, she said, "Wait!" She drew her face in tightly as if mustering all her focus. Slowly, her left knee flexed slightly as she lifted her foot a few inches off the floor. "I can lift my leg!"

With tears streaming, we joined heaven's host in shouting, cheering and screaming our praises to Jesus.

Pure awe consumed us as the miraculous presence of God burned through my friend. Like an eaglet becoming aware that it can fly, she continued to trust the gift of love He was giving her. In a cherished mix of tears and laughter, Aly waved her arms through the air in the universal "attention everyone" gesture. Then, she raised each foot off the deck in slow repetition and shouted, "Look! I can dance! I can dance! Jesus, I'm *dancing*!"

Together, we danced. We jumped up and down. We shouted praises up into the scarlet sky.

Finally, I embraced my friend and then looked into her wet, jubilant face. "And so it begins! Now it's time to share what Jesus has done for you." I then moved toward the stairs and positioned myself to assist her down by the elbow.

She looked at me and flashed a smile of such brilliance that it doused my heart with the same glorious love that was flooding hers. Raising her elbows in silent decline of my offer to help, she said, "We got this!" Then, she lowered her once-dead left leg down to the first tread and jumped off the step so that both feet landed together.

As she repeated this "lower and hop" process down the twenty steps, the hop weakened and the step strengthened. With every step downward, her strides became stronger and more equal. When she reached the bottom step . . . she just ran away.

James and I followed with Rook in tow. We arrived in the ranch main yard just in time to see Rachel catch Aly in a strong embrace. Weeping in pure joy, they danced within each other's arms. Aly continued her exploration of freedom by running up onto the grassy hill. With her arms raised in the air, she looked like the boxer Rocky Balboa—times a zillion—because this was not fiction; a real woman had really been healed.

Looking at James, who was holding Rook by the leash, I nodded my head toward the dog's heavy harness. "He's not going to need that anymore."

James removed the harness and motioned with his arms for Rook to join his "mom." Side by side, James and I watched a grateful dog join his grateful master. Rook bounded in circles around Aly in a "come celebrate with me" posture. A free dog was beckoning his free mom into the leaping dance of the redeemed.

Engulfed by the overwhelming magnitude of the moment, James slumped against my shoulder and started to collapse. I caught him under the arm and followed him awkwardly to the ground. Through sobs of gratitude he repeated, "She's back. I've got my girl back. I thought I'd lost her . . . now she's back. Thank You, Jesus. I've got my girl back."

Alternating between kneeling and standing, Aly continued to worship with her arms in the air. The once broken earthbound eaglet was soaring.

After reuniting in a long hug, Aly and James entered the barn, where the rest of the assembly was already gathered in worship. Aly walked to the front and waited for a pause between songs. Speaking into a microphone, she shared how Jesus' love impacted her once-broken body in such a powerful, tangible way.

But it did not stop there; His love continued to flow over the entire barn full of worshipers, who erupted into a spontaneous chorus of applause and praise. As if this were not enough, there was still more. With Jesus' love there is always more.

Aly had returned the microphone and taken a few steps toward the side door. She was still in front of everyone when she started to laugh and scream at the same time. "My leg, my leg! It's growing, it's growing! I can feel my leg growing!"

Along with those in the front of the barn, I could see Aly's left leg fill her once-hollow pant leg. In that single moment, the ravages of atrophy had been reversed. After it grew two inches in length and four inches in circumference, her leg was restored to its original design and purpose.

Aly left the conference the next day completely healed by Jesus.

When she returned to her doctors, she walked, ran and danced through their offices. Her left leg was subsequently strength tested. Not only did it test stronger than her right leg, but it tested stronger than either of her legs had ever been.

That's what God's wild love does—it restores what is broken to its original design and purpose.

Choosing to Live in the Wholeness of His Love

Jesus not only wants us to know about His love, He wants us to experience it. He desires each of us to be made complete with all the fullness of life and power that comes from God. His love makes us complete. His love makes our lives, our hearts whole.

> Then Christ will make *his home in your hearts as you trust in him.* Your roots will grow down into God's love and keep you strong. And may you have the power to understand, as all God's people should, how wide, how long, how high, and how deep his love is. May you *experience the love of Christ*, though it is too great to understand fully. *Then you will be made complete with all the fullness of life and power*

that comes from God. Now all glory to God, who is able, through his mighty power at work within us, to *accomplish infinitely more than we might ask or think.* Glory to him in the church and in Christ Jesus through all generations forever and ever! Amen.

Ephesians 3:17–21, emphasis added

How easy it is for the hurting to give up in the midst of their dark tunnel and turn away from His loving presence. My dear friend Sarah shared with me recently, "Jesus isn't the light at the end of our tunnel—He's the light *in* our tunnel."

It does not matter if we find ourselves in a tunnel or not, or if we have one leg or two. *He is* with us. His love lights our journey, matching us stride for stride. His uncontainable love for *each* of us draws Him to walk *with* us—every step of the way.

"We know how much God loves us, and *we have put our trust in his love. God is love, and all who live in love live in God, and God lives in them*" (1 John 4:16, emphasis added).

Like an uncontrollable downpour of healing rain, God's love cannot be stopped. It brings life to everything it saturates. It fills and floods everything we lift in trusting obedience to Him. It is not constrained by what we believe He can or cannot do. His love restores legs. His love restores health. His love restores relationships. His love restores whatever broken vessel you invite Him into, especially your broken heart.

God is love. And His love will heal what is broken in you.

Friend, if you are in a place of pain, if your heart feels withered from trauma, thank God—within this place He has provided for you a beautiful choice.

You do not have to remain in your heartache, broken down within your tunnel, viewing His love from afar. You can put your trust in His love and allow Him to flood your being with this truth: "All who live in love live in God, and *God lives in them*" (1 John 4:16, emphasis added).

He is love, and He wants to live in you.

"Let all that I am praise the LORD; may I never forget the good things he does for me. He forgives *all* my sins and heals *all* my diseases. He *redeems me from death and crowns me with love and tender mercies*" (Psalm 103:2–4, emphasis added).

Today, will you allow Him to redeem what is broken within you? Will you allow Him to completely restore you? Instead of a garland of sorrow, you can choose to welcome His strong love and tender mercy to become your new enduring crown (see Isaiah 61:3).

We serve an amazing God indeed. His wild love is the greatest gift of all.

ENCOUNTER HIM THROUGH *Prayer*

Lord Jesus,

With Your wild love, there's always more.

Today, I choose the "more." I don't want to simply know about Your love. I want to experience it. I choose to plunge into the width, length, height and depth of the ocean that is Your love.

Lord, I don't even know what the fullness of this desire will look like, but You do—and I choose You. I don't want to settle for Your benevolent flood to merely lap around my ankles—I want to run and jump into the loving tide that is You. I desire all of me to be immersed in all of You. I ask now that Your passionate torrent would consume me.

I'm inviting You into my broken places. May Your mighty presence drown all that's not of You. Roar into my fractured heart and weakened body and restore all to its natural design and purpose. Lord, let this be the moment You accomplish infinitely more than I might ask or think.

Jesus, You're not the loving light at the end of my tunnel—You're the light of love in my tunnel.

Savior, today, I choose to put my trust in Your love. I choose to open my whole heart wide and receive Your greatest gift—Your all-consuming love for me.

I acknowledge that You Yourself are love, and You want to live in me. You and Your love cannot be separated—they are one and the same. No wonder Your love is the greatest gift of all.

PART FOUR

Encountering His Power

11

Wild Authority

The light shines in the darkness, and the darkness
can never extinguish it.

John 1:5

God is in control. Period.

The wild authority of our God extends far beyond what
we can comprehend. We all seem to know this truth. We often
speak of this truth. But do our lives prove that we *believe* this
truth? If we believed it, we would fear nothing.

The vast scope of His authority stretches light-years beyond any boundary the human mind can grasp. Indeed, He
commands the realms we can see. He stirs the ocean currents.
He orders the sun and moon to follow His chosen course.
He organizes the stars, calling each one by name. He also
commands all that we *cannot* see, the unseen realm of angelic
and demonic power.

I have heard it stated that human nature fears what it cannot control. Yet if this were how God meant for us to live, we would fear everything. Because the truth is, we control nothing except our ability to choose. God did not create us to live in fear. Our fear is contrary to His Word. First John 4:18 (NKJV) states that "perfect love casts out fear"—*all* fear—and guess who "perfect love" is? God Himself.

Where God is, fear is not. Where God is present, the enemy is not.

It is *God* who controls things, not our fears, emotions and circumstances—or Satan.

The enemy wants us to fear him. He wants us to believe in his lies, and every time we do, we give him more power over our heart, mind and life. He cannot *make* us fear him; rather, he suggests that we cower in the presence of his unknown power.

But the fact is, we do know something about his power.

We know that God's power is infinite—Satan's is not. And if Jesus is our Lord, God's Spirit of power and His authority live *in* us. The enemy cannot overpower God in any way, but he can outsmart God's people. That's why our focus needs to be on armoring ourselves with God's Word, not running away from all that the enemy is doing (see 2 Corinthians 2:11; Ephesians 6:10–20).

Jesus is our example in this world. When confronted by the enemy after His forty-day fast—His weakest physical moment—Jesus defeated him with the Word of God. There was no fight. There was no struggle. There was only utter defeat (see Matthew 4:1–11).

Need more convincing? When God engages Satan at the end of this world, there will be no fight, there will be no struggle—there will only be utter defeat by the mere power of God's Word. In Revelation 19:21, John writes that Satan's "entire army was killed by the sharp sword that came from the mouth of the one riding the white horse" (see vv. 11–21).

Our enemy is not all-knowing, but he does already know this—he and his evil hordes are already defeated by the almighty authority of our God. "Then the man of lawlessness will be revealed, but the Lord Jesus will slay him with the breath of his mouth and destroy him by the splendor of his coming" (2 Thessalonians 2:8).

The demonic realm already gets it. Throughout the gospels and Acts we see them recoil when fully faced by those who knew they carried the presence of God within. Our spiritual enemy and his forces already understand and obey the authority of Jesus. Is it not time that the body of Christ does too? Is it not time for us to stop shrinking back in fear and start pursuing that which Jesus has already given His dominion over?

As God's people, when it comes to the spiritual realm, we need to flip the switch in our head and stop playing defense all the time and start playing offense. We already know that we are playing for the winning team—and our dark opponent knows it too.

It is time for us to walk in the confidence of the One who has redeemed us.

By confidence I do not mean pride, arrogance or self-appointed authority—I mean the same confidence that Jesus had when He humbled Himself and endured the cross. Jesus knew this single act of loving obedience would forever break the dark authority of sin and death. Jesus took back the authority the enemy had stolen. He took back what Adam and Eve squandered in the Garden. He took heaven's authority back, entrusting it to us (see Ephesians 1).

It is time for us to walk in the confidence of the *cross*.

It is time to see this world from heaven's perspective and exercise the authority He entrusted to us.

Walking in the Authority of Jesus' Victory

Several years ago, a large local church asked Troy and me to meet with a young woman whom they described as mentally ill. Praying together in the truck, we drove to the designated location where the girl was already waiting. It was a chain restaurant on the east side of Bend, one of the towns near our ranch. We walked through the restaurant doors and into a very disturbing scene. Seated alone in the corner was the young woman we were to meet. Her external appearance mirrored her internal torment.

Her hollow eyes were heavily encircled with thick layers of black makeup that matched her black clothing. Likewise, her fingernails were painted black. Dozens of chained symbols of the occult adorned her neck and wrists. Her face, neck and arms appeared to be coated with something colored in the palest blue, making the pallor of her skin look like a living corpse.

Sliding into the booth across from her, Troy and I engaged in clumsy introductions. My heart clenched as I could feel her dark despair.

Her voice and body shook as she spilled the details of her horrific story. During her childhood she had been sold into the satanic church. Although she looked much older, she shared how she was halfway through her preparatory eighteenth-birthday ritual. She had been groomed for this impending ceremony her whole life, and now it was only two days away. She had full understanding that the final ritual

156

would be her death. In a moment of clarity, she realized she did not want to die, so she escaped from her captors.

Now she sat, shaking in terror before two complete strangers. I reached across the table and placed my hand on her arm. She recoiled in the same manner as if I had laid a burning red fire poker across her skin. "Friend, everything is going to be okay. Jesus has got this, and He's got you."

At the mention of His name, she released an awful groan and recoiled in physical pain. I heard it, and I saw it. She was covered and filled with the enemy's legion. Following the lead of the Holy Spirit, I asked her if she wished to get some fresh air and come sit with us outside. We knew this could get "messy."

Troy held the door open for our new acquaintance, who walked out first. As I walked through behind her, he grabbed my arm gently and nodded toward the girl's back. I understood the volume of what he was silently indicating: This girl had lived her life as "prey"; she would feel safer being approached by a woman. I nodded in full wordless agreement.

Once we were all reseated outside on a shady patch of grass, I began by sharing about the only hope for her—and for all mankind. His name is Jesus.

Again, she recoiled in groaning physical pain. The more I repeated the name of Jesus, the more she looked as if she were being stabbed repeatedly.

"Friend," I began, "Jesus came from heaven and walked this earth. He lived a perfect, sinless life, and then, because of His great love for you and me, He laid that life down as a sacrifice for our sin."

"That's right!" she hissed, her demeanor changing completely. "We killed Him! We killed Him! Jesus is dead!"

Cutting her off with the truth of God's Word, I said, "Then you *know* that He did not *stay* dead. You *know* He rose from the dead after three days. You *know* that Jesus is alive! He is the way, the truth and the life, and *no one* comes to the Father but through Him!"

Shooting right back, she seethed, "Jesus is dead. He's dead! What you're saying is a lie. It is a lie! It is the greatest lie in all history!"

Without raising my voice, I spoke what the Spirit laid on my heart. "The light shines through the darkness and the darkness can never extinguish it. It is Jesus who is shining into your heart right now. You know it's true because the darkness cannot stay where He is."

She blinked a few times. Her face twisted into a hideous expression of fear. Then she shifted again and asked in the trembling voice of a child, "How can I get safe? Where can I go to get safe?" Then what surrounded her diverted attention back to the enemy and his power. She shared in detail all that was going to happen to her and what they would do when they found her.

The enemy was trying to toss a tangible snare of fear over me.

Again, following what Jesus did, I redirected her back to the authority of Jesus. "When Jesus shed His blood, He broke the lock of sin and suffering."

Reeling backward like she had been punched hard in the face, she writhed in pain. "No, not the blood! Not the blood! Don't speak of the blood. Stop speaking about the blood!" And then all that filled her and surrounded her started to scream in terror, "Not the blood, not the blood!"

Sitting cross-legged right in front of her, I held my palm up. "Stop! Listen!" I said.

The evil chorus shrieking out from her silenced itself immediately.

"Beloved, when Jesus shed His blood on the cross for you, His blood covers you and all your sin. It is His blood that breaks the power of sin and death. It is by the covering of His blood that Satan's power is broken forever."

Multiple times the enemy tried to duck and dodge from being seen. Many times he derailed the conversation by trying to turn all focus back to his suggestions of power and harm. But the enemy is no challenge for the Spirit of the living God. The Spirit matched the enemy stride for stride with the truth of God's Word.

Looking confused and exhausted, her eyes focused on mine, and her mouth opened slightly in an effort to speak.

But she was unable to, so I continued, "Jesus has already defeated Satan. You can also defeat him in your life by choosing Jesus to be your new Lord."

Her eyebrows crushed together as she tried to make sense of a new authority, one she had been told all her life was false. Now she grappled with the fact that it was true—because she could feel it.

"Beloved, the only place you can go to 'get safe' is in the arms of Jesus. He's here now. He's reaching for you. He loves you *so much*. He loves you with His very life. He proved that by shedding His blood and breaking the power of darkness and sin over you."

Her lips started to shake. Her corpse-colored face was split by two great teardrops that streaked down her cheeks.

"Beloved, do you want to ask Jesus to save you? Do you want to ask Him to be your Lord? You can. Right here . . . right now. Is this what you want today?"

Then I witnessed within her the last strongholds of spiritual war. She tried to respond through a flurry of yes answers that were stifled by an equal response of mocking no answers. Each alternating reply was followed by her body either leaning toward me or jerking away violently. Her voice also reflected the battle, bouncing between her pleading child's voice and the jeering voice of an enemy who knew he was already defeated.

Cutting through the struggle, the Spirit spoke, *Do you want Jesus?* It was not really a question. It was a life ring thrown to a girl who knew she was going to die.

"Yes!" was the only word that broke through.

I explained to her what prayer is and how, because of what Jesus did, we can speak directly to Him. Understanding that she would not be able to do this without help, I offered to lead her in prayer.

Troy and I reached for her shaking hands. I explained that I would pray a piece of the prayer, and if she wanted what I had prayed, then she would repeat it. Behind our trio, hungry patrons streamed by and the noise of traffic surrounded us. Undeterred, we bowed our heads together on the tiny patch of grass.

"Dear Jesus," I started.

No response.

It took a few false starts for me to realize that the demonic forces still inside her were not going to allow her to speak His name. So with that in mind, I redirected. "Dear Lord."

Thankfully, this was something she could manage, and she followed, "Dear Lord." Piece by piece, she spoke out her need for a Savior. She asked for forgiveness of her sins. She asked for her heart to be washed clean by His blood. She acknowledged that He did rise from the dead, and it was His love that would make her safe and saved.

Finally, at the end of our prayer, it was time for breakthrough, for the last chain to be broken. She needed to declare without wiggle room, semantic bending or demonic mental shuffling who God is.

I finished the prayer with, "Jesus, You are *my* Lord and Savior!"

She tried to follow, but all that came out was a strange sound. "Sh-sh-sh-sh-sh . . . Sh-sh-sh . . . Sh-sh-sh!"

It took me a moment to understand that she was trying to form His name.

Between attempts, her teeth gnashed with guttural growls. But she pressed in. She pursued trying to order her mouth to form a name she had never spoken in her life.

Her repeated effort to speak His name rose in crescendo with her growling and gnashing until her *sh* sound crossed over into *ju*. Her tries became more urgent. "Ju-ju-ju-ju" was punctuated with equally urgent resistance. Between her attempts to speak His name, her growling escalated into throaty screaming, writhing and snapping at me with her teeth. "Ju-ju-ju-ju . . . Ju-ju-jus!"

Fueled by the authority of the love of God, the little girl was winning. "Jusis-Jusis-Jusis . . . Jusis, Jesus, Jesus! . . . Jesus, You are my Lord and Savior!"

Black chains snapped, and an innocent little girl was slingshot into the arms of her heavenly Father.

Her head popped up, and she looked at me with wide, elated eyes. Then I witnessed something I had never seen to this degree before. From beneath her corpse-like makeup, color—a pink flush—formed in the center of her face and spread outward. Suddenly, she jerked backward and started looking at her arms. They, too, were transforming from a deathly blue to a lively pink.

She started to stammer, "It's . . . it's . . . it's on me. It's on me! It's *on* me!" The Spirit of the living God was literally on her, transforming her—every part of her being—from death into life. I believe the revolution I witnessed was seeing with physical eyes the destruction of spiritual evil.

Her face twisted slowly into an awkward expression. Her hands rose to feel the conversion. Pink cheeks started to bunch up as the corners of her mouth lifted in a nearly mechanical fashion. She looked straight at my face as a *huh-huh* sound fell out of her mouth, followed by more. The clumsy sounds strung together to form her first fledgling attempts at laughter.

The fruit of the presence of God was filling her. I can only imagine that what she experienced must have felt like standing under a waterfall of love, joy, peace, patience, kindness, goodness, faithfulness, gentleness and self-control. She was experiencing all these things at the same time for the first time. Like a child taking her first steps into freedom, the result was innocent, awkward and beautiful.

My new friend started to genuinely laugh. She continued to feel her face as it spread into a glorious smile of joy—the undeniable beacon of the redeemed.

The eyes that had riveted on my face were now dancing. Actually, they swam in a jubilant water ballet as tears of joy splashed everywhere. Her hands were still on her face, discovering her new expression, when she came close to shouting, "Look at me, look at me! I'm smiling, I'm really smiling! . . . Jesus did this. He's *real*!"

She was right. Jesus *did* do it. He *is* real.

162

With confident strides, He walked right through all the enemy's strongholds and fortresses for what was His, and He took it back.

Other than a battery of attempted diversions, confusion, threats of harm and superficial posturing, there was no fight. There was no struggle. There was only *utter defeat* of the enemy.

Our time together ended as we waved good-bye, she through a bus window and Troy and I holding hands on a street curb. She wanted to go to her grandmother's house in a neighboring state. Her strong little grammy was the only believer in her family. And she knew that this faithful matriarch had been praying over this day for a very long time. With a single phone call, a stalwart grandmother and her redeemed granddaughter reunited, and a new life for both was ignited.

Abiding in the Confidence of the Cross

> Then I looked again, and I heard the voices of thousands and millions of angels around the throne and of the living beings and the elders. And they sang in a mighty chorus: "Worthy is the Lamb who was slaughtered—to receive power and riches and wisdom and strength and honor and glory and blessing."
>
> And then I heard *every* creature in heaven and on earth and under the earth and in the sea. They sang: "Blessing and honor and glory and power belong to the one sitting on the throne and to the Lamb forever and ever."
>
> Revelation 5:11–13, emphasis added

One of the things that impacted me most on that day was the opportunity to observe the demonic host that tormented this precious girl.

We might not fully understand the power of the name and blood of Jesus, but make no mistake—the enemy hordes *do*.

It was astonishing to see demonic spirits react with intense physical pain and be repelled backward with violent force at the mere mention of Jesus' name. Likewise, the declaration of what broke sin and death's power—the blood of Jesus—sent the evil battalion into a terrified screaming frenzy. They knew all their deception was shattered and they were about to be evicted by the only One who has that authority.

> Because God's children are human beings—made of flesh and blood—the Son also became flesh and blood. For only as a human being could he die, and only by dying could he break the power of the devil, who had the power of death. Only in this way could he set free all who have lived their lives as slaves to the fear of dying.
>
> Hebrews 2:14–15

Jesus is the undisputed Victor in *every* spiritual skirmish. He stated this fact in John 14:30 (emphasis added): "The ruler of this world approaches. He has *no* power over me."

Often, believers—even mature, seasoned believers—react with terror when confronted with the schemes of the enemy.

Well, guess what? The enemy is even *more* terrified of those who carry the presence of God and what they are doing (see Matthew 8:29).

> I also pray that you will understand the incredible greatness of God's power for us who believe him. This is the same mighty power that raised Christ from the dead and seated him in the place of honor at God's right hand in the heavenly realms. Now he is far above any ruler or authority or power or leader or anything else—not only in this world but also in the world to come. God has put all things under the

164

authority of Christ and has made him head over all things for the benefit of the church.

Ephesians 1:19–22

Friend, because His Spirit lives in us, we *can* walk in the confidence of the cross.

We are human, but we don't wage war as humans do. We use God's mighty weapons, not worldly weapons, to knock down the strongholds of human reasoning and to destroy false arguments. We destroy every proud obstacle that keeps people from knowing God.

2 Corinthians 10:3–5

The enemy does not want us to remember this, but the truth is, he cannot even *touch* God's people without God's permission (see 1 John 5:18; Revelation 13). And that permission is given only when it plays into what the Father is already doing.

Think it through. We all recognize and quote Romans 8:28, and this is how it fits: "And we know that *God causes everything to work together for the good of those who love God* and are called according to his purpose for them" (emphasis added).

When it comes to standing in a balanced place before our adversary, I think Pastor Bill Johnson says it best: "I refuse to be impressed with the works of the enemy. I give him only enough attention to line him up in the crosshairs of God's Word . . . *and pull the trigger*. Then I go back to worshiping God."

Above all, you must live as citizens of heaven, conducting yourselves in a manner worthy of the Good News about Christ. . . . Don't be intimidated in any way by your enemies.

This will be a sign to them that they are going to be destroyed, but that you are going to be saved, even by God himself.

Philippians 1:27–28

As believers, when we encounter the enemy in spiritual battle, we need to run *toward* him, not away. Scripture states that our enemy is a coward, and when we confront and resist his attacks, he—not us—will run away (see James 4:7). We are commanded to stand firm and hold our ground when the enemy engages us (see Ephesians 6:10–20).

"O LORD, God of our ancestors, you alone are the God who is in heaven. You are ruler of all the kingdoms of the earth. You are powerful and mighty; *no one can stand against you!*" (2 Chronicles 20:6, emphasis added).

No one can stand against Him.

If Jesus is truly your Lord and Savior, His Spirit, the Spirit of the living God—the same One no one can stand against—rests within you. When we understand the magnitude of the authority our wild God has entrusted to us, we will fear nothing at all.

If you make the LORD your refuge, if you make the Most High your shelter, no evil will conquer you; no plague will come near your home. For he will order his angels to protect you wherever you go. They will hold you up with their hands so you won't even hurt your foot on a stone. You will trample upon lions and cobras; you will crush fierce lions and serpents under your feet!

The LORD says, "I will rescue those who love me. I will protect those who trust in my name. When they call on me, I will answer; I will be with them in trouble. I will rescue and honor them. I will reward them with a long life and give them my salvation."

Psalm 91:9–16

"Now Christ has gone to heaven. He is seated in the place of honor next to God, and *all the angels and authorities and powers accept his authority*" (1 Peter 3:22, emphasis added).

All accept His authority.

Indeed, God is in control. Period.

Everything over, on and under the earth accepts the vast authority of our God. It is time for us to start trusting His authority more than our circumstances. It is time for you and me to not only know this truth but believe it and start walking in His wild, indomitable authority.

"But the Lord is faithful; he will strengthen you and guard you from the evil one" (2 Thessalonians 3:3).

For those who belong to the Kingdom of Jesus, now is the time to stand firm in the confidence of the cross.

ENCOUNTER HIM THROUGH *Prayer*

Lord Jesus,

You said in John 14:30 that the enemy "has no power" over You.

I acknowledge that he had no power over You then, and he has no power over You today. No one can stand against You. All accept Your authority!

Jesus, You are the undisputed Victor in every spiritual skirmish.

When Your Spirit resides within me, the enemy has no power over me either. I don't have to react with terror when confronted with what the enemy is doing in my midst. As a matter of fact, the enemy's even more terrified of me when I carry the presence of my God into what I'm doing.

King Jesus, I commit to You that when I encounter the enemy in spiritual battle, I will run toward him, not away, because Your Word clearly states that he's a coward. When I confront him, he will run away—not me!

When I truly understand the vast magnitude of Your authority entrusted to me, my life will prove it because I will fear nothing at all.

You've not asked me, but commanded me, to stand firm and hold my ground. Today, I choose to start trusting Your authority more than my circumstances. It's not enough to simply know about confidence in the cross; right now I choose to start walking in that confidence.

Reign, King Jesus. Reign through this vessel. Today, I choose to walk in Your indomitable, wild authority, not with my words only but with my life!

12

Wild Goodness

The LORD is merciful and compassionate, slow
to get angry and filled with unfailing love. The
LORD is good to everyone. He showers compassion on all his creation.

Psalm 145:8–9

God's wild goodness. Is there really such a thing?

Whether we call it wild, uncontainable, extreme or untamable, indeed His goodness cannot be corralled or confined
by any human language or perception. All creation echoes
it. The oceans declare it. The dawning sky proclaims it. The
vast wonders of the twilight sky reflect it. All humanity is surrounded by a firmament that mirrors His wondrous, mighty
goodness.

Our God's goodness pours out through His ever-present
willingness to forgive. It streams unhindered through His

love. It gushes forth to all who ask. His goodness is so big that it cannot be contained within itself.

Like the boy who gave Jesus his sack lunch consisting of barley loaves and a couple of fish (see John 6:1–13), what we have might not seem like much in *our* hands. But when we place our meager gifts into the hands of our God, He is the One who can turn our willingness to help others into something amazing, something extraordinary, something *more* than enough.

As He pours out His goodness, it multiplies like loaves and fishes—going on and on and on. His goodness grows in the giving. It multiplies as we take it in and give it out.

Jesus said, "Give, and you will receive. Your gift will return to you in full—pressed down, shaken together to make room for more, running over, and poured into your lap" (Luke 6:38).

Our lives flourish because of, and within, the overflow of His goodness. When blooming in Him, a thriving life begets more life. When we grow within His presence, His goodness multiplies abundant life within us. Out of that abundant overflow, a life-giving river pours into the hearts of those around us—the hearts God has called us to reach for Him.

One of the four pillars that Crystal Peaks Youth Ranch was founded upon is to "Empower the Ministry," to give what we have to help others know God. From the knowing pours the overflow, the sharing of Christ's hope. To "give what we have" should not be confined to certain areas of our life. It should not be held back by our insecurity, pride or fear.

The genuine goodness of our God is rooted in genuine giving. His good giving pours out gifting *wherever* genuine need exists.

The Healing Goodness of Jesus' Name

Not long ago, I took two of my dear friends, Joan and Amy, on one of my favorite hikes. Joan is an old biathlon buddy, and Amy is Troy's little sister, whom I have claimed as my own. Our destination was the Blue Pool, a true wonder of the world according to this wild heart. Draining into the volcanic foothills of the Cascade Mountain Range is the clearest, purest river in the United States, the McKenzie.

This diamond-clear river crashes through several black basalt lava flows. The tumultuous process of passing over and through one of the densest stones on earth purifies the river in a unique way. Because the surrounding region was formed through volcanic activity, it is riddled with lava tubes. At one point, the river makes use of this exclusive method of travel and dives underground for a mysteriously long length of time—some research estimates up to twenty years. The river reappears farther down the mountain, where it roils up beneath a giant black cauldron, chilled down to a heart-stopping 37 degrees. The "bowl" in which it emerges is approximately one hundred yards across and nearly one hundred feet down to the surface of the water.

What I love most about this place is that there is no discernable entrance of the river—but an entire river flows out of the basin. As dramatic as its form is, what makes it such a speechless wonder is the color. From the rim of the cauldron, the water is so clear that it appears to be only 3 to 6 feet deep. In reality, it is 63 feet deep. The water is so pure that it reflects the most surreal color of blue I have ever seen. Although I have tried to capture the color photographically, nothing can compare to the experience of seeing heaven reflected by such a pure canvas. If I could see the Holy Spirit with my eyes, I ponder if He might at times look like this.

Knowing the wonder of how I felt when I first viewed this sacred place, I was excited to share it with my little team. We hiked through the lush green forest that loosely followed the chiseled channel of the river. Our conversation wandered with the same pleasing pattern as the trail beneath our feet. We spoke of friendships, family challenges and how the Lord uses every difficult thing we face to lovingly draw us deeper into His presence.

Nearing our destination, our trio came upon an unusual sight. I saw a woman lying on her back on some soft green moss near the trail. Her elbows were tightly bent with her hands clenched under her chin. On this warm day, she looked cold. Another young woman was standing near the trail, looking in the direction of the trailhead.

Sensing anxiety, I asked, "Hey, is everyone okay?"

The upright woman answered, "Yes, we've already sent some friends out for help. We're going to be all right."

Although she had dismissed me with her best attempt at sounding confident, her voice was not. She was afraid. Recognizing her fear, I slowed my pace to a near stop.

Then the Holy Spirit said, *Look at her!*

I turned and looked directly at the woman on the ground.

She was shaking. A blue ring framed her lips, and her face contorted with pain. She made a low, trembling sound that resembled a hum. Contrary to her friend's words, she was *not* all right.

Sensing the same thing, Joan, Amy and I all stopped at once. I began to slip my pack off when, to my alarm, the recumbent woman's hands began to twist into the rigid, grotesque shapes of someone who was having a full-blown seizure. Her body shook with violent tremors as heavy, anguished moans poured from her mouth.

I declared, "Your friend is *not* all right!"

Immediately, I tossed my pack to the ground, and Joan and I knelt around her. Through a barrage of quiet questions, we quickly learned that the afflicted woman's name was Jan. She was a teacher and was adventuring with her husband, along with a few friends. Her mate was miles down the trail on a mountain bike and unaware of her plight. Two other friends were making their way to the trailhead to signal for help while the lone friend stayed behind to comfort her. We also discovered that Jan had been experiencing flu-like symptoms for three days. With her eyes tightly closed, Jan told us she was bleeding profusely and thought she was six to eight weeks pregnant. She believed she was having a miscarriage.

With intentional calm, I reached into my pack and retrieved a space blanket from my first aid bag. Working together, Joan and I wrapped it snugly around Jan, then placed all our extra clothing over her to combat her rising state of shock. After administering several sips of water, Joan and I lay down on either side of Jan and placed our arms and legs over her to warm her with our own body heat.

Like terrible waves from a nightmarish storm, Jan endured what appeared to be contraction after bleeding contraction. Her clammy body twisted and shook as she alternately hummed and moaned in agony.

My lips were inches from her ear. "Jan, you're going to get through this," I encouraged her. "You're going to be all right. Hold on, girl. Everything is going to be all right." With my entire body wrapped around hers, I said loud enough for only her to hear, "Jesus, we need You now. Will You come, will You heal, will You pour out Your peace in Jan's heart."

Jan's personal storm escalated until she was barely conscious. Her pulse was high and weak.

Fearing she was reaching a physical breaking point, I did my best to quietly coach her to relax her muscles and breathe deeply with an even rhythm.

Without words, she understood and complied.

I was aware of people walking by. A few men were trying to figure out how to construct a makeshift field stretcher. Several folks stopped and looked. Some asked questions, some walked by without a glance.

Like a sentry guarding her post, Amy stood at Jan's feet. I noticed Amy's hands hung close to her sides with palms facing forward; she was praying.

Jan appeared to slip into unconsciousness. There was no more writhing. There were no more anguished sounds. Through my arm across her chest, I could feel her breathing become shallow. The bluish color that previously encircled her lips had now spread across her entire face. Her breaths thinned until they were little more than erratic puffs.

Then, I felt nothing at all.

The rise and fall of her chest ceased. While praying into her ear, I saw her pallor slowly transform from pale blue . . . into a pale white.

By then she was very still.

Amy and Joan's prayers intertwined with mine. I do not remember praying much more than His name. "Jesus, Jesus, *Jesus*! Holy Spirit, breathe! By the power of God, breathe! *In the name of Jesus, breathe!*"

And then . . . *she did.*

Still surrounded by the combined warmth of our bodies, she took a single sudden draw. Then another. Gradually, her shallow draws became deeper and more consistent. Slowly, a normal color returned to her face. Jan's shock appeared to completely reverse. Bit by bit, her body unclenched. The waves of pain had lost their grip. The drawn expression of angst was gone.

As if traveling up through a long dark tunnel, Jan's consciousness was returning. She was coming back to us. After a great heaving exhale, and with her eyes still closed, her lips started to move. She appeared to be trying to dampen her lips. Finally, she whispered in a drifting voice, "Angels . . . angels. You came when I needed you most. You're like angels from heaven."

"Not quite," Joan replied softly without missing a beat. "We're just three women who love Jesus Christ."

Through the combined efforts of several men and Amy's assistance with some accessory cord and two dog leashes, the field stretcher was completed. Once Jan was strong enough to be helped into a sitting position, Joan and I dressed her in the survival clothing Amy pulled from the bottom of my pack. With great care, a chorus of hands moved Jan onto the stretcher. Two men took position at her head, another man and I took her hips, and Joan took the place at her ankles.

Speaking with a gentle voice, I counted, "Three, two, one . . . *lift.*"

Together, our small ragtag group lifted up a desperate stranger on a stretcher made of walking poles, shirts and dog leashes. Then we set off toward the trailhead.

During our hike out, Jan continued to improve. At one point, she was so revived that she sat up under her own power. Then she asked that we stop and allow everyone a much-needed rest. During our break, she slipped out of the survival clothing and folded it neatly. After carefully giving it back to me, she stood up. The savage blood flow that had ravaged her prior had ceased. I watched in awe as a woman—who only moments earlier appeared to be dying—walked the rest of the short distance under her own restored strength.

Only Jesus.

Multiplying God's Goodness into the World around Us

Joan, Amy and I retraced our steps back up the trail to finish our hike. During our trek, we had ample time to ponder why the Lord had allowed us to happen upon a woman in such a critical situation. What did He wish for us to give, to learn, to gain from this experience?

I could not help but marvel at how much this whole situation was similar to the Parable of the Good Samaritan in Luke 10:30–37. We were not the most experienced or the most educated in wilderness survival techniques (one member of our carryout team was a U.S. Forest Service employee, and another was an ER nurse), but of the dozens of people who passed by, we were three of only a few who stopped to help.

Later that same day, we met a man who had walked by, ignoring Jan's plight. We discovered he was a pediatric doctor who was equipped with a thermal mat and a radio, yet he chose not to stop and help. He had everything needed to save her life but inexplicably did not offer it.

I was left to wonder how many times in my *own* life I had done something similar. How many times had I seen someone in trouble, possessed the ability to help and yet walked right on by?

The truth is, each of us has *something* we can give to those in need around us. We may not be the smartest, fastest or best equipped, or have the most experience, but we can stop and give what we have to those who are suffering in our midst. No matter who we are, we can all do that.

But will we?

Or will we mirror the parade of those who walked right by us on the trail without bothering to stop?

We were clearly in need. We were clearly dealing with a mortal situation. Yet all but three walked right on by.

Will we walk right by those who are suffering, even dying, in our midst?

Friend, you and I are not called to walk by. We are called to walk *to*. It is not enough to know the right thing to do unless we *do* the right thing.

"Don't copy the behavior and customs of this world, but let God transform you into a new person by changing the way you think. Then you will learn to know God's will for you, which is good and pleasing and perfect" (Romans 12:2).

I am convinced that without intervention, a bright, beautiful young woman could have died that day on the damp green moss she had collapsed upon. Perhaps she did. But we prayed for the Spirit of the living God to meet her in her distress, and He gave her precisely what was needed to not only survive but to be completely restored.

A week later, Jan contacted me from her distant home to let me know she had just returned from her doctor's office. He could find no evidence of hemorrhaging or physical trauma of any kind. As it turns out, Jan had not been pregnant. All he found was a magnificently healthy woman.

That is the wild goodness of our God!

"You intended to harm me, but God intended it all for good" (Genesis 50:20).

Only by the wild goodness of our God can the evil leveraged toward us be transformed and redeemed into something life-giving.

Surely, we were not the most qualified, educated or prepared. Yet for one suffering woman, what made the difference is that we simply stopped and gave what we had. We gave her the greatest gift—the love of Jesus. And because we serve the King of loaves and fishes, on that day, *He* made this single gift enough.

God will use whatever gift of love you give. He can transform what might seem insignificant to you—once you place it in His hands—into exactly what is needed to save a life.

It is not up to us to understand how God will use our gift. It is only up to us to be willing to follow the example of goodness set by our God and give *something*.

If we choose to give nothing and step over those in need, nothing will happen within our own hearts and the hearts of the people around us, the very ones that Jesus calls us to reach. But if we give Him something, even a little thing, we open the door wide for God to do amazing things through us. Our gifts can be as basic as a card, a gift, a letter, a phone call, an email, a text, a handful of flowers, a hug, a smile or even a prayer as simple as, "In the name of Jesus, breathe!"

"*Taste* and see that the LORD is good. Oh, the joys of those who take refuge in him!" (Psalm 34:8, emphasis added).

God desires us to taste, experience, know His goodness. Within this place, He *will* use and multiply any gift we give Him. He is the Great Multiplier. And His desire is to multiply something beautiful within your heart—and the hearts of those around you.

"The LORD is good, a strong refuge when trouble comes. He is close to those who trust in him" (Nahum 1:7).

Our God is *good*.

Indeed, your life and mine flourish because of, and within, the overflow of His goodness. When blooming in Him, a thriving life begets more life. When we grow in His presence, His goodness multiplies abundant life within us. Out of that abundant overflow pours a life-giving river into the hearts of those around us—the hearts God has called us to reach for Him.

"Praise the LORD! Give thanks to the LORD, for he is good! His faithful love endures forever" (Psalm 106:1).

God's faithful love is everlasting; it endures *forever*. Certainly, the goodness of our God is wild. Together, let's desire His goodness to be wild within each of us every day.

ENCOUNTER HIM THROUGH *Prayer*

Lord Jesus,

You didn't create me to walk by the suffering, but to walk to them. It's not enough to know the right thing to do unless I do the right thing.

I understand that I don't need to be the most equipped in a challenging situation. I only need to be willing to stop and give something to those who are suffering in my midst.

The truth is, I don't ever have enough. But I have You, and You're always enough. You're everything. Because of this truth, it's not up to me to understand how You will use my gifts. It's only up to me to give them.

When I offer any gift wrapped within Your love, it will always be enough. You're the God of loaves and fishes, of flour in the bowl and of rain from a single cloud. When I choose to stop and give Your love, You're the One who makes it an eternal gift.

Today, I purpose to mirror the little boy in John 6 who ran through the crowd shouting, "Jesus, wait! I've got a sack lunch. It's not much, but I give it all." It was small when he gave it to You, but once his gift transferred from his little hand into Your almighty hand, it became exactly what was needed to fill and direct the masses toward Your glory.

I want to give like that.

"Taste and see that the LORD is good. Oh, the joys of those who take refuge in him!" I purpose to pursue becoming a Psalm 34:8 child.

Jesus, right now, I choose to taste, to experience, to know Your goodness.

Holy Spirit, I offer my "sack lunch," my heart, my entire life to be led by You. Release Your wild goodness through this vessel in whatever vast, various, vibrant way You desire.

I'm reaching for Your hand. My love, hope and trust are in You. Lead on, King Jesus!

13

Wild Perspective

"My thoughts are nothing like your thoughts,"
says the LORD. "And my ways are far beyond anything you could imagine. For just as the heavens are higher than the earth, so my ways are
higher than your ways and my thoughts higher
than your thoughts. . . . Where once there were
thorns, cypress trees will grow. Where nettles
grew, myrtles will sprout up. These events will
bring great honor to the LORD's name; they will
be an everlasting sign of his power and love."

Isaiah 55:8–9, 13

Perspective is an untamable thing. A multitude of people
can all experience the same event and yet have completely
different views of their encounter.

Our human perspective dictates that we view our circumstances through the veil of what is best for *our* immediate

needs. We want to be happy, peaceful and comfortable—and that is okay. Few *want* to be depressed, stressed out and in pain. Yet sometimes, our complete upset is the exact stage God uses to move His best plan forward and deeper into our lives.

At times, God allows occurrences in our lives that, in the moment, make no sense at all. Despite our best-laid plans, things still go wrong. Occasionally, they go horribly wrong.

When it comes to perspective, I often consider my love of mountaineering because it has such tremendous correlation to my relationship with God. The higher I go in the mountains, the more powerful the experience. Reaching the lofty heights is where the spectacular views and vast perspectives are most profoundly experienced. But one of the frightening realities of this elevated place is the potential for avalanches. From a distance, they are one of the most beautiful events I have ever seen. Yet when caught up within them, I have a unique perspective. A perfectly quiet, flawless environment can unexpectedly turn into a tumbling, catastrophic disaster.

Life can be like that.

Despite our efforts to maintain balance, life can shift and crack without warning. Suddenly, before our horrified eyes, our peaceful landscape collapses, and we fall in a thundering rampage. Instantly, we get swept up, plummeting downward in a roaring avalanche. We feel as if we are being torn limb from limb. We find ourselves upside down, right side up, bending, twisting, gasping for life. Finally, when the cataclysm subsides, our first discernable breaths tell us we are still alive.

Often, in the unfolding of the crumpled heap at the bottom of the chasm, our first thought, our first perspective is, *Why?*

In that immediate moment of wreckage, we lack understanding. We fail to comprehend the depth of His plan. We cannot receive bedrock verses like Romans 8:28, which promises that *all things* "work together for the good of those who love God."

Good? How?

Instead of falling forward into His waiting arms of trust, we fall backward into the black pit of despair. The longer we stay there, the harder it is to leave. We get stuck in the pain of the moment, fully believing this is our new lot in life. This dark, broken place will become our new home. And this *will* become our truth as long as our vision remains locked on our narrow perspective of the "now."

Thankfully, our perspective has no bearing on His.

Some say that life is like watching a parade pass by. We only see a narrow window, while God sees the entire parade—from beginning to end—all at once. Since He sees everything together, He also sees how it all fits together within the beautiful whole. Because of this truth, we can trust Him with our narrow window, our pile of wreckage. We can trust Him with our rubble, knowing it can never cover His mountain range of reason. We can trust Him enough to stop looking downward at our broken circumstances and start looking upward to the wonder and power of *His* wild perspective.

Choosing to Trust God's Perspective When We Fall

In the early days of the ranch, we rescued a great number of horses. One day, our team redeemed two young fillies: Shamis was a well-built two-year-old buckskin, and Prairie was an unhealthy, underweight, spindly-legged one-year-old chestnut. After many weeks of deworming cycles and supplementary feeding, the two small girls were strong enough to join our young herd in the "baby paddock."

At that time, the ranch was only nine acres, and we were making good use of every inch. The baby paddock was located on the very back of the ranch property. Because our property was previously a cinder mine, the topography of the corral rises sharply to an old access road deeply cut into the cinder pit wall. We have discovered that the steep hill is a wonderful resource in helping to build strength and balance in our rehabilitating horses. We have also witnessed how much fun the colts have playing something that looks like an equine version of King of the Mountain.

As with all our horses, we took every precaution to ensure Shamis and Prairie's safety upon entering a new herd. We allowed weeks of introduction time over a common fence for the two family groups to get to know each other. Through the years, we have learned that the best time to integrate new horses is on the last day of the horse workweek right at dinnertime. The established herd is tired and hungry and less likely to yield to equine drama. So we scattered the evening meal and brought the new fillies into their new home.

Even with hay on the ground, a very kind three-year-old mare named Blessing was unusually curious about her new bunkmates. Wishing only to make friends with the new fillies, she shadowed their every move. Shamis and Prairie were respectful of Blessing's larger size and inquisitive posture. They continued to show submission by slowly trotting away from her forward advances. Blessing proved to be a kind but insistent friend by persistently following the two fillies.

It was Sunday evening, and Troy was off the ranch traveling. All the animals were fed, and the chores of the week were finally completed. Earlier, three of my college-aged staff had joined me in a late-afternoon ride. Now we gathered together to welcome the quiet end of the day and enjoy observing the young horses interact.

My friends and I talked easily as we approached the back fence to climb up, sit down and watch the fillies. Blessing was still in curious pursuit of the new girls as they explored their unfamiliar surroundings by trotting lazy patterns around the paddock.

Suddenly, the little herd took a sharp turn and climbed up the steep hill onto the cinder road.

Interestingly, most horses live their entire lives on a nearly flat surface. So they have difficulty knowing how to initially place their feet or balance their weight when traveling uphill and especially downhill. I have watched young horses try for up to 45 minutes to negotiate their first steep decline.

Shamis and Prairie trotted across the road cut into the side of the pit. As they approached a group of slightly older horses, who did not look too interested in sharing their dinner, the new girls found themselves trapped on the narrow road.

It felt as if I was seeing a slow-motion trajectory of a crash before it happened. I was completely helpless to change the outcome—time, sound, breath stopped. All eyes were on the two young horses moving slowly along one of the highest points of the ranch property.

Shamis and Prairie came to the corner where their only way down was as equally steep as the way they had come up. Sensing this was beyond their experience, they turned around and started walking back the way they had just come.

Blessing was waiting for them. Her ears went forward, and she intended no malice whatsoever. Her only goal was to meet new friends.

As the new girls looked for an escape from unfamiliar horses, they met Blessing face-to-face. Shamis, being a year older, stronger and more confident than Prairie, quickly skirted around the inquisitive mare. Prairie, now alone and being a year younger, weaker and insecure—especially now that she was separated from the only family she knew— began to move her head rapidly from side to side. She was desperately looking for a way around Blessing. In complete kindness, the mare stretched her neck out, extending her nose as close as she could toward the frightened filly. I watched in mounting horror, as I could see anxiety tightening its grip on Prairie.

Finally, in a frantic effort motivated by her own fear, Prairie lunged past Blessing. The mare's nose must have touched the filly's neck as she passed because Prairie jumped to the side.

In what looked and felt like slow motion, her right front hoof started to slip over the rounded edge of the steep hillside, then her left began to slide as well. The weight of her chest and shoulders followed like an anchor going overboard. Even from my distance below, I could see the sheer terror in her eyes as, in one final effort, she jumped.

The only sound I remember hearing was my own heart hammering inside my ears.

I watched in shock. My throat was so tight it felt as if it might snap. I could not move. I could not breathe. I could only stare agape at a little red horse leaping to her ruin.

She landed hard. A sickening, crunchy *pop* shattered the momentary silence that we all stood frozen within.

She was down. And she stayed that way.

"Jesus, Jesus, please help. We need You, Lord. Please . . . help!" The words flew away behind me as I raced up the incline toward the injured filly.

Prairie had landed flat on her sternum with her right front leg crushed beneath the length of her torso. She was wobbling on her hind legs when the girls and I lifted her front end up. Hanging completely limp from the shoulder, her right front leg swung grotesquely free beneath her. Her hoof was no longer pointing forward but directly at her left hoof. Although no compound fractures or obvious breaks were visible, the only thing I truly comprehended was the hideous angle of her leg, which only happens when the shoulder is broken.

She was going into shock. The other horses were approaching. We knew we had to move her to a quiet place. With the combined effort of four women, we eased her down the hill and out of the corral. In our jostled struggle to relocate Prairie, I could see that her useless leg had swung around to a more normal position. Either through shock or habit, I noticed she was trying to put weight on it. My mind whiplashed to times when I had seen horses stand on broken legs.

With our arms, hearts and prayers, we all stood together, holding Prairie up.

After I had finished praying, I left my team and ran up the hill to my home. It was time to make the call—one every horse owner wants to avoid.

Because it was after hours on a Sunday, my plea for help was patched through to an answering service, which, in turn, would contact the on-call veterinarian with my emergency information.

Waiting for the return call from the vet was one of the longest and most personally tormenting moments of my life. I was crushed beneath my own private avalanche of, *if only I had . . .*

Intense guilt rose like choking smoke within my heart. I was suffocating on every angle of this scenario that perhaps I could have somehow prevented. Now an innocent filly's life was going to be forfeited.

188

I was making the call that would end a life.

Alone in my kitchen, I leaned over the sink and gave in to the sobs that roiled up. As I tightly gripped the hair on the back of my head, my emotion poured out into the sink in a flood of gagging tears. A precious little horse had been entrusted to my care, and now she was going to die. In my efforts to free her, I had failed her.

My reeling thoughts spun out into reeling prayers. "Why, Lord? Why did this happen? Lord, I don't understand. Where's the purpose in this? Why, Jesus?" My anguished whispers sounded tinny, inhuman, hollow as they reverberated off the steel sink below me.

Then the phone rang.

I heard a small, firm voice rising inside from a mysterious place of stability. *Stand up, girl. It's time.*

I dried my face with the dirty hand towel by the sink, took a few deep breaths and picked up the phone.

Shay was the vet on call. She was a woman I knew vaguely but liked and respected very much. After I gave her a tremulous detailed recounting, she assured me she was on her way.

I smoothed my hair back, replaced my hat and walked out the front door.

Heavy steps carried me down the footpath toward the spot where I had left Prairie. As I came around the upper barn where we had prayed for her, I stopped.

She was gone.

After a quick scan of the upper ranch, I discovered that the team had moved her into the quarantine paddock over one hundred yards away.

When I walked into the paddock, the girls stepped away from Prairie. She was not only standing on her own, she was now taking tentative steps.

Gears in my brain jammed. Once again, I did the only thing that makes sense among the senseless—our small team of grimy women surrounded the little red filly and prayed.

Shay drove into the main yard of the ranch 45 minutes later. Her demeanor was tense and quiet, which was fitting for the somber job at hand. I updated her with everything that had transpired since our last conversation.

As I debriefed Shay, I was acutely aware of the tools and medications that she was packing into her exam kit. One item was a vial that no animal owner wishes to see. It is the last course of action. Its sole purpose is to end suffering *by ending life*.

I led Shay toward the corral where we had placed Prairie. Inexplicably, the filly was walking more normally—still with a limp but *walking*. After a thorough examination combined with the information we gave, Shay's conclusion was that Prairie had not broken her shoulder but probably dislocated it in the fall. She surmised that sometime during our struggle to move her to safety, the joint was jostled back into position. Shay cautioned that the next 24 hours would determine Prairie's fate. Either the filly would continue to improve, or she would suffer severe nerve damage that would be permanent and irreversible. Our instructions were to keep her as quiet as possible and give her doses of anti-inflammatory medication and antibiotics on a strict schedule.

Thanks to the miracle of Jesus answering our prayers, on this night Prairie would *not* die.

All of us agreed that our Lord must have a greater purpose for the life of this little horse—one yet to be revealed. In guarded relief, the girls excused themselves for the evening and went home.

With my help, Shay began returning her gear to her truck. "She's a lucky girl," she said absently. The tone of her voice was . . . disconnected.

It took me a moment to realize she was not really talking about the horse anymore. Even though she had earlier assured me that the filly would more than likely be okay, it was now clear to me that *Shay* was not okay. When she arrived, I misread her tense demeanor as understandable concern for what she thought was going to be a mortally wounded patient.

The Holy Spirit spoke.

Pursue her. There is more . . . much more.

"Shay, are *you* all right?" I asked quietly, looking right into her eyes.

My friend was silent for a moment before brushing the question off. "You know, the vet on call. No sleep."

I watched her face intently. Even after many sleepless nights, she was still beautiful . . . but greatly diminished. I continued to study her profile. She quickly finished putting her things away. Her hands moved awkwardly in a directionless pattern, like butterflies not knowing where to land. In complete silence, her cheeks began to flush as tears filled her eyes.

Then her face dropped into her shaking hands. Rising slowly from a desperate black place, agonal sounds began to pour over her lips and escape through her fingers. Raw pain flowed out of her soul like scalding lava. Her breathing deteriorated into waves of gasping breaths that crescendoed with the release of soul-wrenching moans.

With my arm around her shoulder, we turned around and sat on the tailgate of her truck. I held her tightly as she wept to complete exhaustion.

When her gut-wrenching waves gradually subsided into ripples, she tried to speak. After a few attempts, she began by whispering, "I've made such a mess of my life."

In the long pause that followed, I thought of all the times in my own life when I could have filled in the blank. While waiting in the silence for her to continue, I prayed, *Lord, on this night . . . keep healing.*

Eventually, she did continue. Her emotionally charged words began to free-fall, gathering momentum, intensity and depth. They obliterated everything caught in their path. They kept falling until her story came thundering down in an explosive avalanche of staggering torment. In the stillness that followed, residual fragments of her life, her heart, her reason for being fell softly like broken snow all around us.

In utter silence, we sat.

The long shadows of evening melted together like black water all around us. Without looking up, her lips parted. There was more—more she wished to say. Her first attempts produced nothing but heavy streaks down her face. Whatever was coming, it was the genesis of her pain, and she needed to say it. The price of holding it inside was costing her more than she could bear.

On this warm evening, I could feel her body begin to shake. My prayer was little more than asking the Holy Spirit to lead into all truth. Indeed, truth was approaching.

Finally, the last fortress of ice fell. In little more than a trembling murmur, she began, "Tonight, I . . . I . . . was sitting on my bed. Nothing made sense. I realized the only way to make the hurt in my heart stop . . . was to make my heart . . . *stop.* When you called, I . . . I was . . . I was holding a gun to my head."

Guilt, anguish, shame and sorrow poured out in one uncontainable gush.

Again, her body writhed and twisted in the grip of one rolling tremor after another. Slowly, her emotion tailed out like an avalanche with nowhere else to go. Her voice was so constricted with grief that it was barely audible. "My decision was made. In all my life . . . I've never needed someone to call me more. And then . . . *you did.*"

I moved my arm from around Shay's shoulders and reached for her hands. I gripped them tightly within my own, and together we wept. Once she started to regain her emotional balance, I turned to face her squarely. Lifting her hands slightly and holding them firmly within both of mine, I said, "Shay, look at me."

I waited until her haggard eyes rose.

"Everything you've shared tonight, all of it, still *cannot change* one simple truth. It is the truth upon which your whole life rests. Friend, you are so *greatly* loved. Nothing that you *feel*—nothing that you've *done*, nothing that's been done to you—will *ever* change that truth. Jesus' love for you is like light in the darkness. And the darkness can *never* extinguish it! Even in this black moment, in all your messy wreckage and pain, He loves you *exactly* how you are *right now.* Will you allow Him to love you? Will you allow His love to come into your pain? Will you allow Him to heal your heart tonight?"

There, in summer's twilight on the tailgate of a dusty truck, two women bowed their heads and asked the Author of light to come into the darkness and redeem. Her beautiful mix of humble, meager, earnest prayers rose through the darkness, binding us together in a powerful braid of pure sincerity. The resulting cord ascended from a shattered heart of flesh, bearing its broken pieces as high as understanding allowed. In return, burning up the blackness as it came, the heart of the Father covered the rest of the celestial distance with the immeasurable speed of a heavenly Dad running to receive His prodigal girl. In a grounding arc of pure white love, tears of hopelessness were incinerated by the infinite flow of the Father's healing compassion for His beloved daughter.

Trusting Jesus' Loving Plan on This Side of Heaven

It was not until I watched the red taillights of Shay's truck disappear into the night that I realized something powerful. Only hours earlier, I was begging God to help me understand why a senseless tragedy had happened to my little horse. In the quietness of the night, His greater perspective was emerging. His picture is always bigger than my narrow view through pain.

"Senseless" only exists on this side of heaven.

God's plan *always* makes sense to Him. Whether we understand it or not does not change this fact (see Isaiah 55:8–9). He *always* knows what He is doing. Our tiny perspective has no bearing on His perfect purpose.

My phone call to end a life became His call to *save* a life.

Unbeknownst to me, my tragedy was needed to prevent an even greater tragedy that was about to happen. There *was* an emergency—an emergency that was bigger than mine. To prevent loss of life, in *that* moment an emergency needed to happen for an emergency phone call to be made.

This is God's wild perspective.

There is always a plan—and He can be trusted for it.

I walked over to the corral where Prairie and Shamis were peacefully spending the night together. Through the darkness, I watched them leave their dinner to come to the gate and greet me. Prairie had improved even more. Clearly, she was going to be all right.

Looking up into the night sky, I could not help but ponder and pray along the lines of 2 Corinthians 1:3–4.

Lord, sometimes You allow us to hurt. When we're flooded with anguish, it rarely makes sense at the time. We pray for release . . . and instead of taking us out of our pain, You go through it with us. During this process, You not only show us who You truly are, You show us who we truly can become. You reveal how our pain can be transformed into something beautiful when it's filtered through Your healing love and poured into the heart of another. Only then do we realize that our hardship has value—not only for us but for the hurting around us as well.

The apostle Peter wrote,

> And through your faith, God is protecting you by his power until you receive this salvation, which is ready to be revealed on the last day for all to see.
>
> So be truly glad. There is wonderful joy ahead, even though you must endure many trials for a little while. These trials will show that your faith is genuine. It is being tested as fire tests and purifies gold—though your faith is far more precious than mere gold. So when your faith remains strong through many trials, it will bring you much praise and glory and honor on the day when Jesus Christ is revealed to the whole world.
>
> 1 Peter 1:5–7

In times of great pain and stress, instead of asking God, *Why me?*, because of His redeeming love, we can ask, *Why not me?*

> Dear brothers and sisters, when troubles of any kind come your way, consider it an opportunity for great joy. For you know that when your faith is tested, your endurance has a

195

chance to grow. So let it grow, for when your endurance is fully developed, you will be perfect and complete, needing nothing.

James 1:2–4

We will be *perfect* and *complete*, needing *nothing*. Certainly, our pain is worth that.

Indeed, there will be times when our complete upset will be the exact stage God uses to move His best plan forward. Most certainly we can expect God to allow things to happen that, *at the time*, do not make any sense at all. Despite our best-laid plans, things will still go wrong. Occasionally, they will go horribly wrong. Yet because of our God's wild perspective, we can trust Him *through* our troubles by knowing He has a plan—a perfect plan. And it is good because He is good.

"So if you are suffering in a manner that pleases God, keep on doing what is right, and trust your lives to the God who created you, for *he will never fail you*" (1 Peter 4:19, emphasis added).

When we choose to trust the perspective of the Holy Spirit, what feels like an avalanche to us can become the beautiful outpouring of the Father's love to another.

Indeed, this is God's wild perspective. Whether you see it or not, you can always choose to trust Him—because He promises to "never fail you" (1 Peter 4:19). And that is a perspective you can count on.

ENCOUNTER HIM THROUGH *Prayer*

Precious Lord,

I thank You that no matter what I face, You've always got a plan. I know things will happen in my life that, at the time, don't make sense at all. Despite my best efforts, sometimes things will still go wrong. Occasionally, they will go horribly wrong. Even so, I choose to trust You through my troubles because I know You've got a plan. And it's good because You are good.

Jesus, I recognize that times are coming when my complete upset will be the chosen stage You use to move Your best purpose forward. Right now, I choose to embrace the fact that my hardship has value—not only for me but for the hurting around me as well. Today, I embrace this truth. I desire Your will over my comfort or understanding.

Lord, when my heart hurts, instead of praying for release, may I rest in knowing that instead of taking me out of my pain, You will go through it with me. By doing so, You show me who You truly are—and who I can truly become.

Your Word declares that You will never fail me, and through my challenges I will be made "perfect and complete, needing nothing" (James 1:4). Certainly my pain is worth that.

I trust You, Holy Spirit, for what feels like an avalanche to me can become the beautiful outpouring of Your love into another.

Because of this truth—today—I choose to rely on You through whatever crush might befall me. Through it all, I choose to embrace You and trust in Your wild perspective.

14

Wild Provision

This same God who takes care of me will supply
all your needs from his glorious riches, which have
been given to us in Christ Jesus. Now all glory to
God our Father forever and ever! Amen.

Philippians 4:19–20

Our God is a wild Provider. His ability to provide supersedes
all our expectations and parameters. Often, our perspective
on provision is limited to the realm of finances. But our
perspective has no bearing on all He provides.

According to Philippians 4:19, God will supply *all* our
needs. *All* is an all-inclusive word. There are no exceptions
to *all*.

In this life we *will* have a great supply of needs, and our
God is wondrously capable of supplying them all. He is a
good Father—the best Father in the history of mankind.

His Son, Jesus, testifies, "If you sinful people know how to give good gifts to your children, how much *more* will your heavenly Father give good gifts to those who ask him" (Matthew 7:11, emphasis added).

I see God's wild provision through Ann, one of my dearest friends. Like me, she is passionate about blueberries. Any day of the year, you can ask her what she would most desire to eat, and her response will always be the same: a giant bowl of blueberries. Even though blueberries grow wild in the mountains of the Pacific Northwest, they are still expensive to buy—in any season. Yet throughout some of her family's skinniest financial times, Ann has shared some of the sweetest encounters of how the Lord has blessed her with an abundance of blueberries.

For some, it is easy to turn the corner of thinking, *Blueberries? Really? Come on, it's just blueberries. I'm sure her blueberry encounters were just coincidental. Isn't that kind of a detail?*

To this I would answer, *Yup. Because God is in control, there's no such thing as coincidence.*

He is a good, *good* Father.

Indeed, God delights in gifting His children.

"From his abundance we have all received one gracious blessing after another" (John 1:16). And Psalm 37:23 says, "The LORD directs the steps of the godly. He delights in every detail of their lives."

Think about it. Even an earthly father provides far more than money for his family. An earthly father also seeks to provide every detail for those he loves. What dad does not buy ice cream for his kiddos? They do not *need* to eat frozen sweet cream, but they do delight in it. What loving father does not cuddle his kids and occasionally toss them into the air over his head? His kids do not *need* to be tossed in the air, but they do squeal in delight every time. If we, in our humanity, understand the power of providing the details, how much more would our heavenly Father?

Paul attributed these words to Jesus: "It is more blessed to give than to receive" (Acts 20:35).

It only makes sense that if our human hearts delight in well-placed provision, God's heart would infinitely more so. When God provides for the details of His children, His Father's heart is doubly blessed. Provision that blesses others while multiplying backward to bless the giver is the template of His genuine giving.

This is the wild provision of our God.

Our Extreme Need Heralds His Extreme Provision

One thing I am learning about growing up is that with age comes the luxury of time lived out—specifically, the ability to look back over a life and see how His provision was always in the mix, matching us step for step. Within this gift of looking back, I have come to realize something beautiful.

The most extreme provision is *always* born out of the most extreme need.

I recognized the dawning of this truth within my life when I was nine years old. At such an innocent age, I viewed my mother as the most beautiful woman in the world. It was also the season in which I believed with all my heart that my dad was a superhero in disguise. I was certain there was nothing he could not do. I was equally certain that somehow he wore an invisible cape and he could fly. I grew up in the combined castle of my parents' love. From my perspective, life was perfect.

200

Until it was not.

On a dark day in February, my dad's best friend came and picked me up at my elementary school. He also gathered my two older sisters. Together, we sat shoulder to shoulder across the back seat of his car. It reeked of cigarette smoke. We all sat in utter silence.

The penetrating stench of cigarettes only added to my ominous sense that something terrible had happened. Oppression hung so thick in the air that it felt like a vise grip on my throat. I could not speak. I could not breathe. All I could do was cower in the terror of the unknown.

Looking for reassurance, I glanced up at my oldest sister's face. She was streaming silent tears. She knew too.

Left to sit in the awful hush of overwhelming dread, we drove a familiar road to our grandparents' house. Once we arrived, I noticed cars everywhere, all parked in complete disarray. I could sense waves of anguish pouring from the house, the same house wherein I had never felt anything but loving refuge.

I stood outside in the driveway, staring at my grandparents' home.

For the first time in my life, I did not want to go inside. I did not want to face the horror awaiting me. Someone grabbed me by the shoulders and pushed me through the door. I was pressed into the arms of a woman I recognized but did not know by name.

She was crying so hard that she was nearly choking. She seemed stuck in a sickening vortex of crying, gasping and repeating how sorry she was. I watched her draw in three quick breaths, then sob out in a stream, "I'm sorry. I'm sorry. So, so sorry." Then she wailed and repeated the whole process—over and over again.

I did not want to hear what she had to say. At this tender age, I did not yet understand that none of us gets to choose this life's great mysteries. We only get to choose who will be our Lord through them.

Finally, the wailing woman blurted out, "I'm sorry. Your father has just murdered your mother . . . and killed himself. I'm just so sorry."

My own voice echoed inside my head. *Wh—what? What are you saying? What are you talking about? That's not true. My dad loves my mom! And he loves me! He would never do that. He would* never *do that!*

"Liar!" exploded from my lips. I popped my hands against the woman's chest and broke away from her embrace. I hit the back door at a full run and kept running in a child's effort to outrun the unthinkable. The short distance felt like miles.

Finally, I collapsed, falling facedown in a small, freshly plowed orchard. My body writhed as I began inhaling dirt, choking and retching through screams.

Then, a single cry rang out. "Jesus, help me. *Help me.* I need You now."

I did not even know who Jesus was. Before that awful day, I only remember going to church twice. All I knew about Jesus was that I was pretty sure He was the guy on the cross. Yet in that crushing pain, I knew He was the only One who could help me.

I begged Him to help me—and He *did.*

Although I did not understand the fullness of that moment, what I did sense was that I was no longer alone. I did have a sudden, unique awareness that everything was going to be okay and that somehow, I would survive.

Looking back, the raw power of verses like Romans 10:13 now makes sense to me: "*Everyone* who calls on the name of the LORD will be *saved*" (emphasis added). It does not matter who you are, how you were raised or what culture you were taught to respect. In your moment of devastation, you can cry out to Jesus.

When my heart was being destroyed, I knew intuitively to turn to the One who made the heart—because I sensed that He was the *only* One who could heal it. And just like that, a child was orphaned . . . and then redeemed.

My sisters and I moved in with our grandparents that same day. Even though they lost their daughter, they saw our gaping need and opened what was left of their family to make a new home for us. As one can imagine, the following decade was fraught with the painful challenges of processing grief.

At the end of that difficult season, I met and married my husband, Troy, the continual love of my youth through this present day. We moved from Redding, California, to Bend, Oregon, following my beloved grandparents' northward migration. Although my grandparents lived to be 90 and 89, they vacated this child's heart far too soon. In their absence, the wide wake they created through my life left an equally wide void.

I loved my parents. I loved my grandparents. Now they were *all* gone.

What remained in their stead was hollowness.

Although God's Word and His Spirit were ever-present in my life, there was still a physical void.

It was my ever-patient mother who taught me how to knit. I think of how much it would have pleased her to see the sweet blankets she taught me to make for loved ones who are welcoming new babies into the world.

My dad was the one who inspired my all-consuming love of snow. After my first Olympic trials race for biathlon, I returned to my room alone and curled up on the wide ledge of the windowsill and wept. All that filled my heart was how much my dad would have loved to have been there.

For years, every May Day heralded the fact that I would never be able to ambush my grandmother with surprise flowers on her doorstep again.

And I have never studied animal tracks in the wilderness and not smiled inside at how much this would have made my dear old Poppie grin.

They imparted such joy, so much so that much of their joy lives on within me.

Indeed, my life is full and rich, filled with joy and peace.

I have adoring "elders" in my life, including Troy's mother and stepfather, whom I love dearly. And I know they love me dearly.

Because of God's immeasurable kindness, I seek and lack nothing. Yet, even still, He had *extra* that He wanted to provide for this girl. Although my life overflows with the continual provision of my God, unbeknownst to me He had *even more* "provision" in mind.

He is a good, *good* Father.

Choose to Walk Out Every Detail with Our Heavenly Papa

After I wrote my first book, *Hope Rising*, our little ranch was contacted by tens of thousands of individuals. Amid the sea of new communications, a single message stood out. It began, "You will not remember me . . . but I will *never* forget you."

Through a phone call, I learned that Katie was a woman of my mother's age. She was a new believer when she heard the tragic news of how my parents died. As a young mother herself, she grieved for the three orphaned girls who were left behind. In her fledgling faith, she did what mattered most—she started to pray for the girls.

All Katie ever understood was that the girls had been taken away. Where the remnants of this shattered family ended up was never made known to her. She prayed for the orphaned daughters for years—decades. Still, never knowing what happened to them, she kept praying.

One day, Katie's pest control man knocked on her door solemnly and gave her a book. "I know you love kids and horses," he said, "so I know you will love this book." Inexplicable emotion rose in his eyes, but before she could really grasp what had happened, he rushed back to his work truck and drove away.

Puzzled, Katie thought in agreement that she indeed loved kids, but she knew nothing of horses. Why did her exterminator drive all the way out to her home only to bring her a book? What about this book inspired a tenderhearted man toward emotion? She was left to ponder what the Lord might be up to.

Fueled by curiosity, Katie started to read the book. Even its title, *Hope Rising*, was no coincidence.

After several chapters, the story took a faintly familiar turn.

"Wait a minute, I *know* this story and I *know* this girl!" she exclaimed to her husband, Larry, as she pointed to the tiny picture on the back cover. "This is Kimmy Caldwell. She's the youngest daughter of our neighbors from Old Shasta!"

Reaching up through the decades from the darkest point of my life, a light broke through, the light of Jesus. And now on the phone, here she was, a warm voice from my past.

"Honey, I want you to know something," she began. "I was your neighbor when you were a child. I knew your mother. We were friends. I want you to know that Jesus loves you so much that *He* has encouraged me to pray for you. I've been praying for you since you moved away from Old Shasta. Kim, I've been praying for you for the last *33 years*."

She continued, "Honey, it doesn't matter how old you are, *every girl* needs a mom . . . and if you choose, I would like to shoulder with what's left of your family and *become* that for you."

Silence.

I fell beneath the weight of *His* love—love that motivated an acquaintance to pray for *me* for *33 years*.

Without my awareness, she prayed that I would receive Jesus as my Lord. She asked God that I would sense His saving grace, His hope, His love, His joy. She asked Jesus to help me find my place in this world—and gain the foundational understanding that even though my parents were gone, I was not an orphan. I was a daughter of the Most High.

Without Katie's knowledge, God had fulfilled her *every* request. Indeed, I met Jesus the day my parents died. I officially accepted Him as my Lord and Savior fourteen months later. In two years, I started teaching Bible studies on the playground of my grade school during recess. The flame of Jesus' hope within my heart gained momentum as I went on to attend and teach youth gatherings through my high school years. Then, I went to a Bible college not far from where Katie lived. I met my beloved husband, moved to Bend, Oregon, and served in several high school youth groups. Undeniably, it was God the Father, Jesus the Son and the Holy Spirit combined who fulfilled the loving role of Father for me.

Finally, I started a ministry of rescuing hurting horses and pairing them with brokenhearted kids, free of charge, sharing with all the redeeming love of Jesus. Over the last 22 years, Crystal Peaks Youth Ranch has gone global, helping to start more than 200 other similar ministries worldwide. My husband and I have been serving Jesus Christ through the ranch ever since.

Katie had no idea how faithful God's provision had been all along.

God waited for His perfect timing to perform a miracle in the form of a book. In a single moment, God allowed her to experience His joy in accomplishing her prayers. It all happened the moment she turned over a book written by a Christian author and saw the tiny picture of a woman on the back—the little girl she once knew.

As soon as the Lord revealed what He had been doing over the last three decades, Katie pressed in even further. "Now that I've found you, I don't want to ever lose you again. I want you to know that you belong to a family . . . the family *He* has chosen."

With that single declaration, the electric current of the Holy Spirit arced between our hearts—and they've been welded together ever since. To this day, we remain in continual communication. She and her husband, Larry, daily pray over the ranch, the ministry, the church and the speaking and writing. She sends me messages filled with her love, support and encouragement. For the last dozen years, she has been true to her every word and true to *His* Word.

Jesus told His disciples, "No, I will not abandon you as orphans—*I will come to you*" (John 14:18, emphasis added).

Without a doubt, He has.

207

I am no longer an orphan. He *has* come, through a loving means that was completely unexpected. His love has provided for this girl's heart in ways she did not even *know* were vacant. He *is* a good Father, and He delights in providing every detail for those who are His.

> Taste and see that the LORD is good. Oh, the joys of those who take refuge in him! Fear the LORD, you his godly people, for those who fear him *will have all they need*. Even strong young lions sometimes go hungry, but those who trust in the LORD will lack no good thing.
>
> Psalm 34:8–10, emphasis added

Again, "those who trust in the LORD *will lack no good thing*" (v. 10, emphasis added). This is not a suggestion—it is a declaration. A declaration of what is *true* about our God. Because He is a good Father, He wants to provide not only what we need financially but *so* much more.

Often, I have quenched the flow of His Spirit to provide merely because I did not invite Him into the details of my life. What Father would not want to provide blueberries for His kids, or a loving family, for no other reason than to participate in their utter delight?

"The LORD God is our sun and our shield. He gives us grace and glory. *The LORD will withhold no good thing from those who do what is right*. O LORD of Heaven's Armies, what joy for those who trust in you" (Psalm 84:11–12, emphasis added).

His *joy* awaits. Friend, I encourage you to invite Him in. Welcome Him into every room, closet, corner and drawer of your heart. Allow *Him* to hear your dreams and desires. Share with *Him* every detail of your life. In the quietness of your place of prayer, reach up to the hand that has always been reaching for you and take a firm grip. It is time to learn to walk hand in hand with your heavenly Papa.

> "Bring all the tithes into the storehouse so there will be enough food in my Temple. If you do," says the LORD of Heaven's Armies, "I will open the windows of heaven for you. *I will pour out a blessing so great you won't have enough room to take it in! Try it! Put me to the test!*"
>
> Malachi 3:10, emphasis added

God wants you to bring your tithes. He wants you to trust Him with every part of your life. He Himself wants to pour out a blessing on you that is so great you will not have enough room in your heart to take it in. He is so passionate about this that He *challenges* each of us to try Him, to put His blessed outpouring to the test.

When we choose to press into His mighty love and take Him up on His challenge, only then will we experience the wild provision of our God.

ENCOUNTER HIM THROUGH *Prayer*

Lord Jesus,

Your Word states that those who trust in You will "lack no good thing" (Psalm 34:10). This is not a suggestion but a declaration—a declaration of what's true about our heavenly Father.

Lord, You said, "I will pour out a blessing so great you won't have enough room to take it in! Try it! Put me to the test!" (Malachi 3:10). I recognize that I haven't put You to the test. I haven't invited You into my dreams, hopes and desires. Instead, I've relegated myself to what I can see, to the here and now, to the mundane things of life. I've bowed my heart to the world's faithless mantra of, "It is what it is."

Precious Lord, I don't want to keep living adrift in "whatever" land. I desire to pursue Your "purpose" land. Today, I welcome the truth of Your Word: "Blessed is the man who trusts in You!" (Psalm 84:12 NKJV). Your joy awaits entrance into my being. You want to fill every part of me with Your beautiful, powerful, sweet provision of joy.

Right now, I invite You into every room, drawer, closet and cupboard of my heart. You know what I need. You know what to fill these hidden places with. Even when Your provision initially seems painful, I will trust You—for as long as it takes—for my pain to be transformed into Your joy.

In this moment, I let go of the complacent realm of, "It is what it is." I choose to trust You to walk me into Your presence, the place of Your wild provision, the place where I will "lack no good thing." I'm reaching for You, Lord. It's time for me to walk hand in hand with my heavenly Papa.

PART FIVE

Encountering Him

15

Wild Encouragement

Be strong and courageous, all you who put your
hope in the LORD!

Psalm 31:24

We live in a fallen world that is dominated by sin.

If we fail to calibrate our focus on the truth of God's Word
every single day, we can become disheartened, sinking into
the mire of discouragement—a tool, a weapon of war that
the enemy uses to distract and confuse God's people. It is
not glamorous, but it *is* highly effective.

One reason why discouragement is so efficient in derailing
believers is because it usually begins in such an innocuous
way. It is the traveling partner of fatigue and nearly always
waits until our defenses are weakened by exhaustion. Once
our hearts are tired, it lays a single straw across our weary
backs, and then another and another. Each straw, each

negative suggestion from the enemy, is weightless, power-less on its own. But when we allow the lies of our foe to pile up on our weary heart, it often does not take that much to fracture our resolve.

Our deepest discouragements are enacted by the enemy through those we love and trust. When the levy of our heart is breached, when our love is wounded and our trust is broken, discouragement floods in like a black torrent. Its primary purpose is to extinguish the flame of *truth* within us. Once this dark deluge overwhelms our heart, our focus breaks away from Jesus' beautiful face. As we turn our attention from the light of His glory, all other views become dim beneath the gloomy tide. With nowhere else to turn but our own waning strength, we collapse into a rising sea of shadowy deception.

Raw discouragement always sweeps us away from our Lord's plan.

It is not a fruit of the Spirit. It is not from God. Instead, it appears as a tiny black dot, a dark presence so small, so apparently harmless that we often do not feel threatened enough to instantly brush it away. Then, when we recognize and challenge this negative blot as not innocent, it rises into its true form—a towering monster that can take down most in a single bite.

Yet as powerful as discouragement is, Christ's encourage-ment is a zillion times more so.

When we know *who we are in Jesus*—and actively practice our relationship with Him—discouragement has nowhere to hide.

"So be strong and courageous! Do not be afraid and do not panic before them. For the LORD your God will person-ally go ahead of you. He will neither fail you nor abandon you" (Deuteronomy 31:6).

God's Word is true. He will go before us. He will *not* fail us. He will *not* abandon us.

When we learn to stand on the bedrock of His Word, this is where we experience the wild encouragement of our God.

The Perfect Placement of Our God's Wild Encouragement

Troy and I were working down to the tail end of a long speaking tour. Our second-to-last stop was at a very large urban church. This was an evening service and was designed to reach a millennial crowd. While exhaustion from the heavy schedule stalked us both, we were still excited for the opportunity to speak in this venue.

Upon arrival, we meandered the empty campus, looking for someone who could direct us to the right building. Although we never found anyone, we did eventually find the correct location. We stepped into the large auditorium just as the worship team was assembling for practice. In moments, it was abundantly clear that they were extremely talented. They flowed seamlessly from one powerful song to the next without any distractions.

While listening, my awareness pinged off something—something nearly intangible. There *was* a distraction.

Even though nothing was said or done to indicate tension, I sensed a brittleness among the worship team. This rigidity streamed out with the music that poured from their mouths. Although the worship was beautiful and skillful to my ears, it left my heart empty. I was aware of an aftertaste, an essence that was not to be savored, that was not cohesive with the Spirit. My sense was merely an observation, not a judgment.

215

I moved toward the sound booth in the back of the building. After a few moments, I caught eyes with the sound man and then waited. Fully aware that worship practice had begun, I did not want to interrupt, but I did want to respect those who had previously instructed us to be ready and on time.

Once the team had played through several more songs, he looked down at me from his operations booth and muttered, "Who are you?"

I explained that we were the speakers for the evening and we had been instructed to meet him at this time for a sound check.

His emerging expression was unmistakable. He was annoyed. Then he pointed at the exit door on the back wall. "You can wait outside. I'll send someone out for you later." With that, we were dismissed to go stand outside.

So we obeyed and stepped out into the oppressive, humid heat normally found in the region. In minutes, we sweated through the only clothing we had with us. I was already feeling sorry for everyone who might wish for a hug from me later in the evening.

Finally, the door cracked open, and an anonymous hand motioned for us to come back inside. More than happy to oblige, we stepped back into the coolness of the building. The sound man handed me a wireless battery pack and headset and motioned for me to go to the stage.

Trying to respect the time frame given us, I put the gear on as I made my way up and onto the massive platform. I counted to ten a few times aloud and saw his thumb go up in the very back of the room. Not really knowing where to go from there, Troy and I went to the opposite side of the back row and took the two seats closest to the door.

Long moments went by. I noticed a few members of the worship team reappear and move toward the exit doors behind us. Sensing their phantom heaviness, I stood up and casually encouraged them as they passed.

Their response made my heart sink. Apparently, I was a phantom as well. They walked past without stopping or speaking. One member turned toward me and tossed his chin in the air and made a *huh* sound. That was it.

What washed over me in their passing wake was not heaviness, but pride. I recognized its thin masquerade from earlier years of my own life—years when the Lord had entrusted me with a special gift. It was a gift given from Him—to be used *for* Him. Sadly, in my immaturity, I often applied this unique ability for my *own* satisfaction.

Although this worship team was currently a "performance" team, I value the fact that we each have our own rare journey of maturity before Christ, which is good—because He is good. Every prideful, fearful, fumbling step that we take becomes a single valuable piece within the picture of the whole in which we will become.

At last, the event coordinator arrived. Her demeanor was bright but apologetic. She explained that the pastor who usually spoke on this night would not be attending. Apparently, an argument arose between them about us coming. It became so sharp that he refused to have anything to do with this event. That single wave of information gave more understanding as to why this whole process had been so tumultuous. Prior to our arrival, we offered to send books to support the event. Although this church had a large bookstore, they refused our offer despite our making it abundantly clear that while traveling and speaking we do not sell the books—ever. We give them away for free.

This place appeared to want nothing to do with us. Yet here we were by invitation, inadvertently adding fuel to a contentious fire set ablaze before we arrived.

Soon, crowds started to pour in through the doorways and fill the seats. On cue, the worship team reassembled and began their set. The room darkened, and a dazzling array of lights danced over the assembly while they sang. As moving as the scene was, my heart struggled to focus on worshiping the One I serve.

In the same moment that I allowed my gaze to drop, I could hear the enemy's accusations.

They don't want you here. None of them wants to hear what you've got to say. Look around! This is a trendy, hip millennial crowd . . . and you're none of those things! Look at your stupid clothes! You don't fit here! You don't belong here! You're not even wanted here! They don't value you! They don't care if you go, so just go! Leave! Leave now!

Amid the pulsing crowd, my exhausted heart plummeted. My knees followed the downward spiral as I silently sank to the floor. Tears streamed down my face. My shield was down. My sword was down. My strength to stand was trampled beneath the dancing feet all around me.

In a final act of survival, I reached up for the only life ring that can save, speaking His name: "Jesus, Jesus, *Jesus*! I need You now. Help me to stand up and walk through what You're calling me to do." Still collapsed on the darkened concrete floor, I—an exhausted woman, a girl soldier—waited in weary expectation.

From somewhere high above, I could sense His Spirit approach. Like an eagle coming in for a landing on its master's outstretched arm, His words landed with precision in the middle of my heart: *"Don't be afraid. . . . Take courage! I am here!"* (Mark 6:50).

Jesus said this to the disciples, who thought they would die in a ferocious storm. In a single, simple statement of fact, He declared that He is in control. He is with us. He has already won every battle we will ever face.

Don't be afraid. . . . Take courage! I am here!

If I knew, and believed, no other verse in the Bible, this single declaration of truth would be enough to see me through *all* of life's challenges.

After long moments of resting in His presence, my heart moved toward recalibration, redirection, restoration. The worship set was winding toward conclusion. It was time. I dried my face, rose to my feet, straightened my clothing and made my way toward the stage.

I shared all that Jesus had laid on my heart. Nothing was held back, softened or diluted. Romans 10:13 is true: "Everyone who calls on the name of the LORD will be saved." I urged those in attendance to give Jesus their heart—*all* of their heart. Even if what remained of their life was broken pieces, He would take that too, because He is the only One who can redeem what is broken within us.

I handed the stage to Troy, and he also shared with Spirit-inspired passion and truth. At the close of the message, we were told that someone would come up and offer an invitation to all who were moved by the Spirit to receive Jesus as their Savior. Once onstage, instead of pressing into the sacred moment of the Holy Spirit, that individual shifted gears and took on a "game show host" persona, opting for product giveaways in place of the invitation.

My heart sank.

On that night, no opportunity to receive Jesus or to move deeper into His Presence through prayer was offered.

Then, the indoor portion of the event concluded. Everyone was invited to stay for continued fellowship in an expansive outdoor courtyard where refreshments would be served. Troy and I were swept along in a sea of faces all crowding toward the next phase of what felt like a colossal party. We were encouraged to stay as long as we wished. Within moments, a large group crushed around us outdoors. Troy and I ended up standing back to back, each ready to pray with anyone who desired.

But no one wanted to pray.

Instead, we were surrounded by those who wished to tell about their own relatable experiences. Although sharing personal connections is not a bad thing, it was not the primary reason we had traveled so far. It was not the King's best thing. My heart waned as I scanned the throng around us.

Lord, is there not even one who wants to pray?

Then, I noticed him.

He stood quietly behind multiple rows of those who encircled us.

I smiled at him, indicating that I saw him and wanted him to stay.

He returned the smile with a slight nod that told me he understood. He was patient as he waited and waited . . . and then waited some more.

I was intrigued by what could be so important that he would linger so long to speak to us. Finally, it was his turn to share what was on his mind.

Once he stepped fully into my view, I had a chance to place my complete attention on him alone. He had a strong stature and was slightly shorter than me. His tanned face was framed with rich, curly black hair. His short beard and mustache only accentuated the beautiful lines of his smile. In any culture, race or region, he was handsome. Yet far more striking than his appearance were his eyes. They were deepest brown and shone with a rare, indefinable laser-like brilliance. When he looked directly at me, I could feel the presence of his gaze. His shoulders supported a well-used backpack, and his feet were shod with simple worn leather sandals.

He reached for my hand. "My name is Jason," he said.

While holding my hand in both of his, he looked into my eyes. There was an unusual power in his gaze, an undefinable clarity. Then he did something completely unexpected. Still holding my hand, he drew me in and slid his left hand beneath my hair against the nape of my neck. After letting go of my hand, he cupped my cheek with his right palm.

As he pulled me closer, what I felt could best be described as . . . *electrocution.* My mind froze. I could not move. I could not speak. Still cradling my neck and cheek in a supremely tender embrace, he positioned my ear only inches from his lips.

Then, with deliberate purpose he spoke.

"I've been sent . . . to thank you . . . for speaking on behalf of our King."

Slowly, he pulled back so we stood eye to eye. What felt like shock waves pulsed from his hands through my face, my mind and down my spine. White-hot current arced across my heart. In an instant, I had the sensation of melting and fusing. Recent and old images incinerated into a liquid form that reassembled in new configurations. In that fraction of a second, I felt a transformation, something like blocks into bridges—where truth had been blocked, it now flowed. The current continued to race through every nerve bundle and branch until it ignited my feet, welding them to the concrete upon which I stood.

Our eyes remained locked—only twelve inches apart. After what felt like days, he smiled a peaceful, knowing smile and leaned back to his full arm's length. Gently, he pulled both of his hands away at the same time. While holding them slightly above my shoulders, he wordlessly rotated his palms up. His expression deepened into a smile so dazzling that it was hard to look at—but even harder not to.

Totally mesmerized, I tapped my husband on the shoulder without breaking my gaze. When he turned around, all I could say was, "Troy, this is Jason."

Then, like watching a mirrored image, I saw Jason do exactly the same thing to Troy. He held my husband's hand within both of his. Then, he reached up and placed his left palm on the nape of his neck and, releasing his hand, placed his right palm on Troy's cheek. I witnessed a small, brilliant-eyed man draw my six-foot-two husband into the most compassionate male embrace that I have ever witnessed. Although I could not hear the words spoken, my husband's changed expression clearly spoke for both.

There was the same lingering gaze that was followed by the same ever-brightening smile. Suddenly, there was a bump from behind. A gentleman had tried to step around us through the crowd and accidentally stepped into us. Although his apologies were profuse, none were needed. Through spontaneous laughter, we made jokes about our size and how neither one of us made a very good doorway. After a shared moment of whimsy, we embraced the dear soul, and he went back into the fray.

Quickly, we turned back to Jason, who was nowhere in sight.

I looked up at my husband's astonished face. I then glanced in the direction of where we had parked the rental car hours before. Without words, we moved through the crush. Reaching for my hand, Troy took the lead, and I dropped in behind him as he maneuvered us through the mass of humanity with great care. Our mincing steps stretched into full strides. As soon as we broke free from the pack, we ran hand in hand all the way to the car.

After we jumped in, we turned toward each other in mirrored unison. "Do you think he was real?" we asked simultaneously.

In adrenalized excitement, we both started talking at once.

My first intelligible blurt was, "His eyes! Oh, my goodness! Have you ever seen anything like that? They actually had a . . . a . . . feel! In all my life, I have never had a stranger embrace me like that."

Troy added, "I know! That was so crazy intimate. Had he not been twice my size, I am not sure I would have allowed him to hold my face!"

My mental gears jammed. "What? What do you mean by 'twice your size'? Jason was not even as tall as I am."

Now Troy was the one with jammed mental gears. "Jason. You know, the Jewish-looking man with the black curly hair, tight beard, backpack. He was huge! He towered over me. His hand was so massive on the back of my neck that he was touching both of my ears at the same time. When he reached out to grab me, my first thought was, *Do not fight this guy! He could bend you into a pretzel without even trying!* I just knew I was supposed to yield."

I could feel my eyebrows mashing together in confusion. "What are you talking about? Jason. The super handsome Jewish-looking man, black curly hair and short black beard, backpack, brilliant eyes. He was barely *my* height! We were

223

nearly the same size in every way. Because he was an unimposing stature, I wasn't intimidated to receive such a compassionate touch."

In our garbled debrief, we discovered that the man we encountered embodied what we each needed to embrace his gentle "laying on of hands" and to receive his message. I experienced a super gentle, beloved little brother, and Troy experienced a super masculine, admirable big brother. Apart from his perceived size, our experience with Jason was identical.

"I've been sent . . . to thank you . . . for speaking on behalf of our King."

My heart will never be the same.

God's Wild Encouragement in *All* Its Beautiful Forms

Looking back on that day has forever changed my perspective on verses such as, "Keep on loving each other as brothers and sisters. Don't forget to show hospitality to strangers, for some who have done this have entertained angels without realizing it!" (Hebrews 13:1–2). Presumably, there have been a multitude of times when we have been in the presence of the host of heaven and we did not realize it. Yet every now and then, *we do.*

Sometimes God answers our pleas for help in astounding ways. Sometimes He speaks to us through His Word or through our family and friends. Often, He will encourage us through worship music, books and teachings, physical signs and wonders, and—sometimes—through staggering encounters with "strangers."

He is a good, *good* Father, and He always speaks to us in the language we understand. Because I am a woman of the wilderness, He speaks to me everywhere I go through the vast and wild creation of His hand.

Lately, His vehicle of encouragement has been eagles— bald eagles. While I am praying, pondering or problem solving, they appear—sometimes circling high above, sometimes perched in silent wisdom atop a snag, sometimes skimming the treetops, screaming as they go. Indeed, they are a part of this world, and some could relegate their rare presence to coincidence. But what I am learning about the wild encouragement of our God is that if you look for it, you will always find it . . . in all its beautiful forms.

My dear friend Sarah shared with me, "You always know when something's from Jesus. Even the hard things become good because—in the end—He always wants *for* you instead of *from* you."

Spoken another way, the challenges of this life are what drive us into the deep places of intimacy within the very presence of our living God—the same God who declares over you and me, "Don't be afraid, for I am with you. Don't be discouraged, for I am your God. I will strengthen you and help you. I will hold you up with my victorious right hand" (Isaiah 41:10).

When it comes to encouragement, it is God Himself who holds us up.

"Therefore, since God in his mercy has given us this new way, we never give up" (2 Corinthians 4:1).

What more do we need to know? The wild encouragement of our God is all around us all the time, because *He* is all around us all the time. *He Himself* holds us up no matter what we face. And if we take the time to look, really look for His encouragement, we will always find it . . . in *all* its beautiful forms.

ENCOUNTER HIM THROUGH *Prayer*

Lord Jesus,

Thank You for the beautiful intimacy of encouraging me through the language I most understand.

I'm simply in awe of Your loving support that runs like a perpetual river through my life. I know that if I look for Your encouragement, I will always find it, in all its astounding forms.

I recognize Your Spirit's presence in my heart, the One who continually wants for me—instead of from me.

It is You who declares over me, "Don't be afraid, for I am with you. Don't be discouraged, for I am your God. I will strengthen you and help you. I will hold you up with my victorious right hand" (Isaiah 41:10).

There is no mistaking this fact: You Yourself hold me up.

"So we can say with confidence, 'The LORD is my helper, so I will have no fear. What can mere people do to me?'" (Hebrews 13:6).

Precious Savior, what more do I need to know? Your wild encouragement is all around me all the time—because You are all around me all the time.

Today, I choose to believe Your Word. Today, I choose to trust in You more than my fear. Today, I choose to stop depending on my circumstances and start depending on Your presence for every ounce of life-giving encouragement You wish to pour into my soul.

Today, precious Savior—for this reason alone—my heart will never be the same!

16

Wild Courage

Be on guard. Stand firm in the faith. Be courageous. Be strong. And do everything with love.

1 Corinthians 16:13–14

The wild courage of our God beckons. Borne forth on the
breath of every breeze, it calls us. It summons us through
each sunrise. His wild courage invites us with every drawn
breath, with every heartbeat to step through the veil of our
cloudy, limited understanding into the vast realm of His limitless understanding—and *trust Him*.

At its core, God's courage is not fearsome but loving.
When we understand the depth of His love for us, courage in
Him becomes the natural overflow. Courage is not something
we work to produce—it is the by-product of fully trusting
in Jesus' love.

His love for me inspired His courage to endure the cross. His courage to endure the cross inspires my love for Him to overflow into the beautiful action of sharing the Gospel.

Paul summed up this truth in Acts 20:24: "My life is worth nothing unless I use it for finishing the work assigned me by the Lord Jesus—the work of telling others the Good News about the wonderful grace of God."

Courage in God is not passive. It does not sit on the sidelines of battle wringing its hands in the hope that everything will turn out all right. Righteous courage moves us into *action*. Motivated by Jesus' example of love for us, we move forward, fueled by His love in us for the lost around us.

When the fuel tank of our heart is filled with God's love, combustion of His compassion within us creates courage.

Simply stated, God's love and His courage cannot be separated. Each fuels and moves the other into action.

Stop Acting like Prey, and You Won't Become Prey

Crystal Peaks Youth Ranch has assisted in starting and shouldering with over two hundred similar ministries. We serve hurting families, primarily with horses. This "church planting" through ranch ministries has drawn us to travel across the United States, Canada and around the world. Spending time in the support and encouragement of these ministries abroad fills our hearts with the wonder of the Holy Spirit. We are constantly inspired by what He can do anywhere through anyone who dares to say yes to Him.

My husband, Troy, and I were once invited to Colorado by one of our similar ministries. After assisting them with a fundraiser and touring their lovely ranch, it was time to go deeper. As much as travel schedules will allow, we always try to make room for private time with each of the ranch founders. Within these sequestered moments, we follow the Holy Spirit where He wants to lead. Often, it is within these personal occasions that the strongholds of the enemy are identified, prayed through and broken off. This is my favorite part of every encounter—seeing God do what only *He* can.

Although our friends had fully utilized every inch of the ranch that had been entrusted to them, its location was beyond the reach of any major population. This nullified much of their work because those who needed their ranch most lived too far away to access them. With proximity in mind, our friends had located a piece of property about thirty minutes northwest of Denver. Our personal time together took the form of joining them for the day to prayerfully walk over the property and seek the Lord's will.

Although the drive was beautiful, our conversation was anything but. While winding up through the mountains, our friends shared a horrific tale. Another local family had chosen to shoulder with them in their ranch ministry. Both families had children, and both had fourteen-year-old sons. In a single devastating moment, the supporting family's son believed that the best way to solve his problem was to take his own life. At fourteen, he was still a boy.

I watched one of my dear friends collapse under the weight of grief and confusion. Hot tears of anger poured down her face as she recounted, "I will never hug my son again and not grieve for their loss. They will never hold their son. They will never meet his wife. They will never cradle his babies. We were all watching, and we never saw this coming. The enemy just stole him right out from under all of us, and I'm just *so angry!*"

When we reached our destination, the mood was somber. We dried our faces and stepped out of their car.

The property lay in stark contrast to our solemn state of mind. It was beautiful. Resting at approximately 8,500 feet, steep grassy slopes swept around tall stands of stately ponderosa pines. The red-sided conifers gave way to multiple groves of quaking aspen. Various wildflowers waved among the assembly. Each variety added their own unique step to creation's perpetual dance of praise.

This property was magnificent. Every boondock cell in my wild heart rose to its feet and started cheering along with this powerful place, giving glory to the One who made it. Slowly, wordlessly, our group of four split apart. We each moved as the Spirit led.

My love of the wilderness was implanted early in my life. My dad was also passionate about the wild places. He was a downhill ski instructor on Mount Shasta and taught me his love of snow at the age of four. Our family was raised in Northern California near Whiskeytown Lake. In the summer months, we frequented this blue diamond many times a week. I also learned how to water-ski at the age of four. Likewise, with my little hands planted firmly in the back pockets of my dad's 501 Levis, he towed me up my first peak, 10,463-foot Mount Lassen, when I was five. While I was still young enough to count my age on one hand, my feet were firmly placed on a wilderness path, a path they have never left.

My dad died a few short years later. But what he instilled into my heart lives on. The baton of imparting the love of the wilderness had been passed on to my grandfather, who became my legal guardian and took care of me for the next ten years. My beloved Poppi was a true mountain man. He was a hunter, a fisherman, a trapper and a skilled teacher of all these things.

He was the one who taught me how to read my environment, to "see" the perpetual message board of the earth. Our surroundings speak to us all the time. Every track, every scrape, every detail of who had been here, what they did and where they were going fascinated me.

When I became a fledgling archer, he counseled me to be very aware of my opponents.

He told me that when I encounter bears, I should look down, turn a quarter shoulder and casually redirect my path. Moving in this manner is bear language for, *You're the boss. I'm no threat to you. I'm yielding to your authority. And I'm just going to be on my way.* My grandpa was right. In my explorations, I have come across many bears, and his counsel is sound. Some stood up, some grunted and most ignored me in a "huh, no harm, no foul" kind of way. Each bear encounter has been amazing.

Most importantly, he instructed me to be aware of another apex wilderness predator—the mountain lion. He told me that unless I was about to be killed by one, I would never see a lion. They are among the deadliest feline killers on earth. Their kill rate is among the highest in the world because they are stealth predators that always attack their prey from behind. Their vertical jump can launch them fifteen to twenty feet straight up. Their horizontal leap has been measured at an astonishing forty feet. An ambush predator, they leap on their victims from behind while biting the back of the neck. The vertebrae of the neck are crushed or the carotid arteries are pierced. Either way, the prey dies at almost the same moment it realizes it is being attacked.

When Poppi told me this, my incredulous expression told him in return that I might never enter the woods again.

In his deep, quiet voice, he reassured me that every lion is a coward at heart. Outside of a few extremely rare occasions, they will vehemently avoid all human contact.

But if I ever *did* encounter a lion face-to-face, Poppi's instruction was to hold my ground. Maintain fierce and direct eye contact. Make myself as large as possible by holding my arms over my head. And most important of all, do not, do not, *do not* back up—*ever*. I am sure my sky-high eyebrows told him that more reassurance was in order.

"Don't worry, kiddo," he said in his signature baritone voice. "If you don't act like prey, you won't become prey."

Because of that voice of authority, which resonates in my heart to this day, and the experienced education that accompanied it, I came to see the wilderness not as a fearsome place but a blessed place. In its purest form, it is my sanctuary, my church—the place where I experience the wonder of God.

This day was no different. Released on a Coloradan slope, I set about to explore the glory of this world as led by His presence. Soon, I came to a deep crease in the earth. I noticed it was made by flowing water—a very good thing in this drought-plagued region. I then followed the path of the phantom waterway down into a fallow grove of aspen trees. Indeed, to my surprise, there was a small pool of residual water. And . . . there was something else.

My ever-scanning gaze locked onto a rare sight—an antler tine was rising through the duff on the forest floor. Only members of the deer species shed their antlers every year. In this nation, that is narrowed down to moose, elk and deer. To walk up to the very place where antlers are shed in the vast wilderness is extraordinary, even when you are looking for them—which I do everywhere I go.

I smiled at God. Finding an antler is so rare that, for this heart, this event becomes a covenant moment between the Father and His girl every time.

He tells me in a voice that I recognize, *Whatever you're praying about, whatever you're pondering, whatever is pouring through your heart in this moment—here's My covenant with you. I've got this!*

Because of their symbolism, antlers are a big deal to me. Even though many adorn my home, each one is symbolic of a covenant He has spoken over my life.

I reached down to pick up the treasure and discovered that there were actually two—a perfect pair. The antlers were very dark and glossy. They were large and heavy. Clearly, they came from a beast of a buck. This boy was so big you could have *ridden* him. While freeing them from a heavy layer of pine needles, I noticed something else: These big, beautiful antlers were not shed—they were still attached to a skull. This buck had died after being taken down by something more powerful than itself.

Although I wanted to keep the antlers, the Lord let me know that this was a covenant He wished to make with my brokenhearted friends. Calling out to them, I delivered the trophy and the message of hope it represented.

Returning to the virtually dry waterway, I continued my curious search to see where it might lead. Soon, I was well beyond calling distance of anyone in our party. Lost in thought and prayer, I meandered, vaguely following a path where water had once flowed freely.

Always scanning my environs, I saw it. Jesus is such a fox. Off to my right, near the base of some brush, another antler tine rose above the grass. I laughed out loud. It was an elk antler—the first one I had ever found. The antler was a small five-point of about two feet in length.

"Lord, thank You!" was my instant response.

Even though I know elk can travel up to twenty miles a day, I still searched the immediate area in hopes that this bull was bedded down and the matched pair would be close by. Sure enough, the second antler lay on the other side of the brush. I raised them both in complete wonder, acknowledging how ridiculously *rare* this moment was.

Amid my outpouring of praise, a single thought shot through my heart.

Jesus, this is way *more than a covenant. What are You trying to tell me? Speak, Lord!*

Listening intently, I walked on in silence. My course shifted, and I was now pressing upward, on to the shoulder of a steep ravine.

What happened next is difficult to describe.

Suddenly, I felt as if I had stepped under a roaring waterfall of imagery and information. Rising over the fray was the voice of my King.

I . . . am . . . so . . . angry! The enemy has moved into My land. He is attacking My people. He is killing My children. Enough of his attacks! I am calling all those who are Mine to stand up and fight! I am calling My people to take back the land My Son gave His life to defend! Rise up, My people! Rise up and take back the land! Take back the land. Take back the land!

My mind flooded with impressions of ancient wars. Massive clashes of hundreds, thousands of horses and riders charging into battle. The collision of opposing armies was deafening. Sparks flew as swords and shields crushed against each other in mortal combat. Verses, words, parts of messages, eagles and rushing water all poured together into an epic moving scene.

There was a brief profile of a man looking up. He was watching a colossal wall of immeasurable proportions. As massive cracks exploded through the wall from the top downward, the immense fortress began to yawn outward; the wall was coming down.

Out of nowhere came a voice. Its shout cut through *all* like a laser beam. It embodied the definition of authority and roared, *Looooook!*

I felt it as much as I heard it. Not unlike contacting a wild electric current, every fiber of my being stiffened in the shock wave.

I bolted straight up.

Then I saw it. Not ten feet away in my nine o'clock position was a bush that had been bent over by long-receded winter snows. And beneath it crouched in full attack position was . . . *a mountain lion.*

Its eyes were so dilated with excitement that they looked completely black with only the narrowest ring of gold circling the outer rim. The lion was coiled like a mighty spring compressed tight to the ground. It was waiting for me to take one more step—the last step that would put the predator behind me, the final step that would make this a true ambush.

The crush in my head evaporated instantly before this very real foe. Everything spun down into what felt like slow motion. As if slogging through mud, my brain could barely make sense of what my eyes were seeing.

This really is a mountain lion. It really is targeting you for its next attack.

My mind flashed over all the weapons I carry in the wilderness under normal circumstances. But I had come from the airport the day before; I had nothing. My prayer rose as a single thought.

Jesus, I've got nothing!

The response was beyond instant.

Yes . . . you . . . do! Raise up the weapons of war that I have given you! Raise them up and fight!

The antlers.

In a single motion, my hands flew up over my head, each fist brandishing an antler. With the lion's gaze locked on mine, a single line echoed through my heart.

I see you. I see you! . . . I see you!

Without conscious thought, I hissed at my enemy.

And it hissed back, its unspoken voice seething with primal truth.

And I see you . . . and I'm going to kill you!

The terrain where we were engaged was very steep. With eyes still locked, arms still raised, I could feel my feet carefully maneuvering onto the highest position above my foe.

The lion's body whipped around, following our unbroken gaze.

The cliché of seeing your life flash before your eyes now makes sense to me. Indeed, there was a parade of random, ridiculous and profound thoughts: recalling my grandpa's counsel, being aware that I was currently hiking in airport shoes with three-inch heels, telling myself that my friend Sue would think this was so awesome, and acknowledging that my husband was *never* going to believe this before actually calling out his name twice.

What could have been no more than seconds felt like long moments. Finally, the realization dawned that I could not lower my arms and I could not back away. Even more, I now understood the three-word Peter prayers. Mine was exactly the same.

Jesus, what next?

His immediate response was equally brief.

Attack! Attack! Attack!

Within His answer there was no gray, no debate, no uncertainty—only His command.

What felt like scalding lava rose in my throat. It could not be contained by logic, culture or reason. The sound that came out of my mouth was unrecognizable. A primal, throaty growl exploded into a terrifying scream. It was the cry of one creature engaging another in a lethal clash. Moving the raised antlers forward and down, I closed the gap between the lion and me with two quick lunges.

My screaming charge brought ten poised, sharp antler tines to within three feet of the lion's eyes.

To my surprise, guess what the lion did.

Nothing! Absolutely nothing! It called my bluff. It only crouched tighter to the ground.

In that instant, a single flash of a moment, something shifted. I was no longer staring down into the adrenalized pupils of a mountain lion but into the eyes of sin itself—my own sin.

The darkness lurking around my heart seethed in a dripping hiss.

You've always known that I've been here. You've just never seen my face until today. You're not really going to drive me out . . . because you like it that I'm here. You're going to keep ignoring me, pretending that I don't exist. You're going to turn your back and walk away. And then I'm going to kill you!

Realms collided.

The enemy's icy lure sent a chilling wave over my being. I felt frozen, paralyzed. Then ice met fire, holy fire. The hostile trap sent over me ignited one thing—anger. Righteous fury welled up like a boiling geyser and exploded in a dominion-shattering truth.

Liar!

Consumed by the inferno, I felt my body surge forward with the intention of driving the tines through the lion and into the ground. Inches before contact, the lion slipped horizontally to the side. I missed. The tines hit the ground hard.

The mountain lion leapt away from me and bounded down the steep slope. Jerking the tines out of the earth and back up in a "reload" position, I watched its escape. As it fled downhill, the tip of its tail swept in huge circles, like a waving white flag of surrender.

"We use the weapons of righteousness in the right hand for attack and the left hand for defense" (2 Corinthians 6:7).

The mountain lion disappeared from my view.

I was left standing on a steep shoulder in a ravine with an elk antler still raised in each hand. Realization started sinking in. I was trying to draw in deep breaths, but my chest was so tight that it would not expand. My hands were shaking *hard*.

The antlers no longer looked like weapons of war but willows blowing in the breeze.

With unfurrowed eyebrows, I blinked multiple times as my mind tried to catch up with the reality of what had just happened. Through the trembling tangle of recognition, a single banner of truth rose and waved above the crush: Jesus won—Satan lost.

Standing on a little knoll by a bent bush, I raised shaking antlers toward the sky and shouted with the host of heaven,

"Jesus, Jesus, You reign! You're still mighty to save! Jeeeeeeee-sus! Mighty is the Lamb!"

Choose to Live in the Truth of Jesus' Victory

The truth is, Jesus always wins and Satan always loses.

Read 1 John 5:4–5: "For every child of God defeats this evil world, and we achieve this victory through our faith. And who can win this battle against the world? Only those who believe that Jesus is the Son of God."

As children of God, *every* one of us can win *every* battle when we stand on faith, believing that Jesus is the Son of God. Need more proof? Read the gospels. Read Acts. Read Revelation. Jesus Christ has already won *every* battle we will *ever* face. Now is the time to start living as if we believe that is true.

Friend, the call on your life is simple. It amounts to three things—only three. Love God, love each other and share the hope of His redeeming love (see Mark 12:30–31; 16:15).

As straightforward as this is, we often fall into every pothole of confusion and misdirection known to mankind. With almost no effort at all, our enemy suggests that somehow we are not doing it right. Then begins the hyperattention on all that is us—our junky past, our failures and mistakes—and forward momentum in the Spirit is completely quenched.

Indeed, if we act like prey, *we will become prey.*

All the knowledge of God's Word in our life is *worthless* if it does not motivate us into action.

In his shotgun style of communicating, James says it best: "Faith without works is dead" (James 2:26 KJV). If we do not trust the leading of the Holy Spirit enough to step out into our unknown, we will never experience His *all-known.*

When it comes to living within the wild courage of our God, there is *no way* to advance before Him without actively living what we believe. God created us to know Him and pursue a growing relationship with Him daily. Out of that relationship pours the overflow, the river of His love that joins us to Him and each other. Out of this beautiful torrent flows the Great Commission, not the great suggestion.

We all have a job to do—a commissioning fueled by the forces of heaven, a spiritual assignment that will be opposed at every step by the forces of hell.

But Jesus did not leave us ill equipped. He is our example. When He was confronted by the enemy through Peter, His response was simple: "Get behind Me, Satan!" (Matthew 16:23 NKJV). Why behind? Because Jesus was moving forward. Jesus commanded the enemy to go where He Himself never would—backward in retreat. Jesus was focused on one thing: advancing the will of His Father. He was advancing the saving truth of salvation. He was taking back the land.

Now is the time to do the same—take back the land of your own life.

Search every part of your heart, examine every secret place where sin could slither in. When you see the eyes of the enemy, advance and drive him out. Defend the heart that Jesus died for.

Now is the time to take back the land of our families. Has sin entered your home through the internet, video games, television, social media, books, movies, music or friends? Parents, advance and take it back. Drive the enemy out of your home. Defend the lives Jesus died to redeem.

Now is the time to take back the land of your community. Are you living and speaking of the hope you believe? Advance and drive the enemy back with love. Defend those around you whom Jesus died to save.

Now is the time to lift up the weapons of war that Christ has given you and use them for His glory. These weapons will be as diverse as every soul who calls Jesus Lord. For some, your weapon of war will be your laptop. For others, it will be a broom, a cell phone, a kitchen, an office, the cab of a truck or a battered minivan with crushed-up juice boxes mashed under the seats.

Clearly, even a set of antlers will do the trick. If you are struggling to know what your weapons are, remember this: *all* of us have two hands—if not physically, emotionally—and *all* of us can put them together and pray. Lift up what Jesus has given you and take back the land!

"Stay alert! Watch out for your great enemy, the devil. He prowls around like a roaring lion, looking for someone to devour. Stand firm against him, and be strong in your faith" (1 Peter 5:8–9).

We are commanded to *stand firm* against him, and *be strong* in our faith.

There are so many things that I love about this verse, but right now, what I love most is the word *like*. Our enemy is "like" a roaring lion, but he is *not* a lion. He is a cowardly ambush predator that lures his victims with lies. Satan might start the fight, but *Jesus Christ always finishes it!*

If Jesus Christ is your Lord, then you serve the Lion of Judah, the Lamb of God, the coming King, the Bright Morning Star . . . the Alpha and Omega. He *is* the Victor. He has already won. He always finishes what He starts. And if you keep your focus on Him alone, He will finish what He started in you as well.

Taking back the land will mean something unique for each one of us.

What lies within your heart that stands in opposition to a deeper relationship with Jesus? Is Jesus really first? If not, what is? Are you willing to drive out the enemy in *all* his forms? What lies within your family that is preventing a closeness with each other, a closeness with the Lord? Parents, is your example leading your family closer to Jesus—or further away from Him? Within your sphere of friends and acquaintances, is your presence leading them toward the hope of Christ—or away from it?

Beloved, this life is not about our earthly comfort. You and I were redeemed to bring *His* comfort to the lost around us. We are alive today to love God, to advance the saving hope of Jesus and to fight for those in our midst who are losing their battle for hope. Jesus is calling you and me to follow Him, to run into the flames of this world and pull out those in proximity who are *burning alive*—toward the saving grace of Jesus Christ.

> You must have the same attitude that Christ Jesus had. Though he was God, he did not think of equality with God as something to cling to. Instead, he gave up his divine privileges; he took the humble position of a slave and was born as a human being. When he appeared in human form, he humbled himself in obedience to God and died a criminal's death on a cross. Therefore, God elevated him to the place of highest honor and gave him the name above all other names, that at the name of Jesus every knee should bow, in heaven and on earth and under the earth, and every tongue declare that Jesus Christ is Lord, to the glory of God the Father.
>
> Philippians 2:5–11

Throughout history, millions of believers have died so that you and I would know the salvation of Jesus. If we call ourselves by His name, the baton of faith has been firmly handed to us. Now it's *our time* to run the message of the Gospel forward through history.

Are we? Is His love so alive in us that we are daily compelled to reach the lost in *any way* Jesus moves us to?

> Then I heard a loud voice shouting across the heavens, "It has come at last—salvation and power and the Kingdom of our God, and the authority of his Christ. For the accuser of our brothers and sisters has been thrown down to earth—the one who accuses them before our God day and night. And they have defeated him by the blood of the Lamb and by their testimony. And they did not love their lives so much that they were afraid to die."
>
> Revelation 12:10–11

The motivation to share our faith does not rise from courage but love. Jesus' understanding of God's love gave Him courage to endure the cross. Jesus' courage to overcome the cross is our promise of God's enduring love. God's wild love begets His wild courage. God's wild courage begets His wild love . . . *for each of us.*

"Again he said, 'Peace be with you. As the Father has sent me, so I am sending you.' Then he breathed on them and said, 'Receive the Holy Spirit'" (John 20:21–22).

Jesus knows us so well. His final encouragements to you and me were precisely chosen. *Be at rest*, He says. *I am sending you out fully armed, locked and loaded with everything you'll ever need.* And yet, within the ranks, some read this commissioning and feel anxious.

Anxiety can only happen when our hope is genuinely in the wrong thing, not in Jesus. Perhaps you have been in and out of church most of your life. You have read the Bible. You have gone to the home study groups. Maybe you have even led them. You can quote Scripture and sing worship songs. You know all *about* Jesus, but you have never *experienced* Him as your Lord—the true centerpiece of your heart, the reason you exist.

What a big difference—an *eternal* difference!

Perhaps this flutter of anxiety is the moment you realize, *I know about Jesus, but I don't know Jesus in a personal way. I'm tired of standing alone. I'm tired of being mauled by the enemy. I'm tired of fighting.*

Friend, no matter where you're coming from, there *is* hope—and His name is Jesus. His loving hand is reaching for you now. Let *now* be the moment you choose to reach back.

If this is your desire—to ask Jesus to come into your heart and be your Lord—all of heaven's host and this author are rejoicing with you. Something beautiful happens in our hearts when we choose to put our body in a position of humility before God. So if you are able, get on your knees before the One who loves you most.

ENCOUNTER HIM THROUGH *Prayer*

Dear Jesus,

I need You now. I've been the lord of my life for a long time. My leadership has led my heart into darkness. My life is broken beyond my ability to repair it. I'm afraid. I realize that I'm a sinner and I cannot fix or forgive my own sin. My sin separates me from God—and this is a darkness that I can no longer bear.

Jesus, please forgive me of my sin. Please wash away my guilt, shame, pride and fear. Please heal all that is broken within me. I receive the salvation only You can give. You are the one and only risen Lord and Savior—and I choose You now.

Dear Jesus, I'm asking You to be the Lord of my life. Holy Spirit, I invite You to come in and fill me to overflowing with Your presence.

Jesus Christ—today—I declare that You are the Lord of my life. From this moment forward, I commit to live every day in pursuit of You. Thank You, Jesus! Amen.

17

Wild God

Our God is wild. It is true.

He palms the universe. He breathes stars. His voice shakes all creation. He divides oceans. He commands the same oceans to consume His enemies. He holds back rivers and releases them at will. He tells the sun to rise and set—even stop—when He chooses. Our wild God is a consuming fire. Jesus told a Samaritan woman this:

> The time is coming—indeed it's here now—when true worshipers will worship the Father in spirit and in truth. The Father is looking for those who will worship him that way. For God is Spirit, so those who worship him must worship in spirit and in truth.
>
> John 4:23–24

The flame of His presence, His Spirit, He Himself is looking for anyone who will worship Him "in spirit and in truth."

It is time to choose to trust *Him* more than our knowledge, experience and emotions. It is time to get out of our own way, our own human logic, and stop leaning on our own understanding so we can worship Him how He wants to be worshiped. It is time to make Him first.

On this day . . . will you?

Pursue the Mighty River of His Power and Presence

I love how our amazing Lord is so gracious, so compassionately detailed in His communication with those who are His. Jesus speaks to each of us in the individual "language" that we understand most clearly. I learn through what I see. So it is no coincidence that He speaks to me continually through His creation.

Not long ago, I was praying in one of my favorite places, a tiny room on stilts upon the highest rim of the ranch.

From this hallowed place, the ranch, the valley below and the majestic Cascade Mountains beyond fill the scope of what human eyes can see. Few are the words spoken in this sacred place that have not been in the form of prayer to the One who redeems.

During my prayer time, the Lord allowed me to see something astounding. Whether I was dreaming or awake remains a mystery to me.

What I witnessed was water pouring down from heaven in the form of a mighty river that flowed with unfathomable volume and power. It was the most magnificent river in all creation. All other rivers known to mankind are mere threads in comparison. Its unstoppable authority rumbled out of heaven and down into the realm of mortals. It struck the top of a monumental mountain and thundered down its flank in a deafening roar. The river poured into a mighty ravine, a hallway of pure stone. It crashed and collided against massive walls of rock as it careened toward its destiny.

Thundering down to the foundation of the mountain, the river channeled its way into a deep canyon spanned by an immense stone dam. As the colossal torrent slammed into the dam, it exploded straight up into the atmosphere. The spray washed through heaven and showered the entire earth.

In that moment, I could hear the voice of my God speak.

Release Me . . . release Me . . . release Me! You were created to release all that I Am through all that you are! Open the doors of your dam by opening the doors of your heart. Choose to pull back your human understanding and let Me roar, roar, roar through you!

Beloved, release Me! Release My power. Release My presence. Release all that I Am into all that you face.

This same vast river mirrors the Spirit of heaven. He moves, pouring from the throne of the Father with unimaginable power and love.

He Himself is crashing—right now—against the doors of your heart, asking for full release.

On this day . . . will you?

Will you choose to pull back the doors of your heart—the doors that slide so easily on the tracks of your flesh?

Will you willingly move aside your logic, your will, your comfort, your fear and your pride and let all that He is roar through you?

As mentioned in the introduction, God is not interested in our "spiritual tourism." He did not intend for us to admire His beauty and glory, power and strength from a safe distance; He created us for fellowship—to want to know Him, to want a relationship with Him more than *any* other thing. He did not conceive us to solely know about Him; He created us to be *filled* with Him and His mighty river.

None of us can truly know God if we are content to roam the edge of His love. None of us can experience the depth of His presence as long as we keep opting to stand ankle deep in the river of His Spirit.

He fashioned us to choose Him. He desires each of us to pursue Him through every door that closes us off from His glory. We were not made to stand in the shallows of His love, but to dive deep into Him. He desires for us to immerse *all* that we are into *all* that He is.

As our Father, He does not want us to stand back and observe Him from a distance. He longs for us, His children, to break through every barrier of our human limitations. He wants us to run toward Him with abandon and trust, then jump into His arms—into His very presence.

On this day . . . will you?

Do Not Be Faithless Anymore—Believe!

After Jesus conquered the cross and rose from the grave, Peter went to His tomb. But he did not stand at a distance and observe it. He did not allow the chains of his guilt to stop him. His many failures, even denying he ever knew his King, did not prevent him from breaking through into greater closeness with his Lord. In pursuit of God, Peter went *inside* the tomb. He walked into the cavern of death with boldness—and found life. *That* is when he believed (see John 20:3–9).

When Jesus approached Mary Magdalene, she was so overwhelmed by her sorrow and her circumstances that she failed to recognize her God. It was not until Jesus *called her by name* that she recognized the voice of her Savior. She did not allow the chains of her grief to stop her. Once she knew it was Jesus, she did not stand back and welcome Him from a distance—she pursued Him and literally ran and jumped into His awaiting arms. *That* is when she believed (see vv. 11–18).

After Jesus rose from the dead, He also appeared to His disciples where they were hiding in fear.

> "Peace be with you," he said. As he spoke, he showed them the wounds in his hands and his side. They were filled with joy when they saw the Lord! Again he said, "Peace be with you. As the Father has sent me, so I am sending you." Then he breathed on them and said, "Receive the Holy Spirit."
>
> John 20:19–22

But Thomas, one of the Twelve, was not there. He told the other disciples, "I won't believe it unless I see the nail wounds in his hands, put my fingers into them, and place my hand into the wound in his side" (v. 25).

Eight days later, when Jesus encountered Thomas, He encouraged His doubting friend to pursue his faith through his skepticism. "Put your finger here, and look at my hands. Put your hand into the wound in my side. Don't be faithless any longer. Believe!" (v. 27).

Once Thomas touched Jesus' hands and side, he did not allow the chains of disbelief to stop him. *That* is when he believed.

Friend, if you are bound by any human chain of guilt, grief, doubt or pride, you have a choice—right now—to pursue Jesus *through* it all. You have the choice to recognize your Savior and not simply know about Him, but run and jump into His presence. The voice of your wild God beckons you to *choose* Him over *all* other things.

Jesus calls to each one of us, *Don't be faithless any longer. Believe!*

On this day, will you fulfill your own unique and beautiful disciple's journey by pursuing a *wholehearted* relationship with Him? Today, will you commit *all* of you—your heart, soul, mind, strength—to be immersed in *all* that He is?

Right now, His arms are open wide . . . for *you*. Jesus Himself is calling your name—His son, His daughter—to pursue Him despite the bonds of your past, snapping them as you run, and to dive into the all-consuming presence of His love.

He is calling you to be *fully present* in His presence.

Let this be your run-and-jump moment when you choose to "clothe yourself with the presence of the Lord Jesus Christ" (Romans 13:14).

On this day . . . will you?

"I pray that God, the source of hope, will fill you completely with joy and peace because you trust in him. Then you will *overflow with confident hope through the power of the Holy Spirit*" (Romans 15:13, emphasis added).

Indeed, when you *fully trust* in God, He becomes your only true source of hope, joy and peace. From this unstoppable river of trust, the power of the Holy Spirit will overflow through you into *your* world—a tide of His redeeming hope.

Beloved, you were designed to be a river, not a lake. You were created to be a pursuer *in* Him, not an observer *of* Him.

Because of all that Jesus has already done, this is the foundation, the bedrock of your relationship with Him. He is

calling you to jump into the relentless river of His Spirit . . .
and experience His untamable presence.

In this moment, He is beckoning you to pursue your wild
God without limit or measure—to encounter and embrace
Him.

So . . . on this day, *will you?*

ENCOUNTER HIM THROUGH *Prayer*

Dear God,

My precious Father, my beloved Jesus, my powerful Holy Spirit, I beg You to burst the old wineskins of my awareness of You. Please break down the barriers of my logic, my understanding, my experience and my emotions—all the things I'm tempted to trust more than You. Right now, I willingly lay my sin before You, asking that You forgive me and remove it all.

Wash, renew and fill my heart and my mind with Your presence and Your truth. Open my eyes to see anything that's not of You and that might quench the mighty river of Your power and presence, so You can fill me and flow through me. I commit today to stand and fight against these things. No more "back doors" that lead away from You.

Come, Holy Spirit, come and fill all that I am with all that You are.

May Your presence be so heavy upon me that there would be no difference between where I end and You begin. May the Kingdom of my wild God fill me so completely that Your presence will pour through my life, lighting up the world around me for Your glory. May those who are suffering in my midst see Your light shining through the darkness and come running into the warm liquid presence of Your healing love.

I choose to remain in Your beautiful presence, knowing that it's only from this place of being in You that Your Spirit flows out of me. From this day forward, may Your amazing overflow through me translate into

*the simplicity of committing to be a "pray, listen, do"
child of the almighty King. May I choose to rest in the
truth that my calling in this world really is that simple.*

*Precious God, be high and lifted up within my heart—
always!*

*To You be all glory, honor, power and praise forever!
Amen.*

Kim Meeder is the cofounder/CCO of Crystal Peaks Youth Ranch, a unique ministry that rescues mistreated horses and pairs them with hurting children, encouraging all toward the healing hope of Jesus Christ. The ranch was founded in 1995 and serves thousands of kids a year, all free of charge. Kim's first book, *Hope Rising*, inspired the ranch to win the national Jacqueline Kennedy Onassis Award and launched her inspirational speaking ministry. She remains passionate to share *complete freedom* and wholeness in Christ by following the leadership of the Holy Spirit. Together, Kim and her husband, Troy, have helped to establish over two hundred other similar ranch ministries throughout the United States and Canada, and a dozen in foreign nations. Kim and Troy have been married since 1983 and enjoy living in Central Oregon.

Facebook: facebook.com/crystalpeaksyouthranch
Instagram: instagram.com/crystalpeaksyouthranch
YouTube: youtube.com/user/crystalpeaks1
GooglePlus: plus.google.com/u/0/+Crystalpeaksyouth ranchOrg